Cooking with the Horse and

JUST
You & Me

400 Amish Recipes for just the two of us

Wayne & Wilma Yoder

ISBN 978-1-933-753-42-3

Book Design: Valerie Miller

Printed in the USA by: Carlisle Printing

Carlisle Press
WALNUT CREEK

800.852.4482
2673 Township Road 421
Sugarcreek, OH 44681

1–82014–5000
2–92015–5000
3–32019–2500
4–102019–2500

Dedication

To all my cooking friends, known and unknown. From beginners to well seasoned cooks, whether you're cooking for one or two.

Pick out a recipe or two and give it a try. You don't need a whole lot of kitchen gadgets to whip together a dish or a meal.

Thank God for your talents, and smile when you do the dishes.

JUST YOU AND ME

Introduction

Here it is, just for the two of you. I'm wrapping up *our Just You & Me Cookbook* after countless hours of creating and altering dishes in my kitchen.

Our daughters, Diane, Leanna and Mabel, helped prepare hundreds of dishes. My husband, Wayne and our son Robert filled their much needed role as taste testers for the new dishes.

All glory and thanks be to God for giving us the patience and strength to work on *Just You & Me* for the past 17 years.

As a couple, Wayne and I want to welcome you to our new cookbook. We enjoyed preparing our favorites for you. We hope the space you give our new cookbook in your kitchen will be worth it, for those times you need to cook for *Just You & Me*.

All recipes marked with were created using the art of "Made from Scratch Cooking". In Made From Scratch Cooking, you take basic items found in your pantry, fruit cellar, freezer, or garden. Mix in a dash of this and a piece of that. Stir in a cup of imagination, then season to your liking. Before you know what happened your kitchen is filled with the aroma of a family favorite in the making.

All recipes marked with have become special family favorites.

JUST YOU AND ME

Table of Contents

∽❧ JUST YOU AND ME ❧∼

Appetizers, Beverages & Dips

Ham Salad

1 c. finely-chopped ham or bologna
½ c. chopped pickles (sweet or dill)
½ c. Miracle Whip
1 hard-boiled egg, chopped

Mix everything together and spread on crackers. You can also put it on a piece of bread and eat as a sandwich with lettuce and cheese. Adjust the flavor by what kind of pickles you use, more or less Miracle Whip, or add some pickle juice. Hard-boiled eggs are optional. If there are any leftovers, it keeps better if hard-boiled eggs are omitted. Create your own taste. Check at the deli counter, usually they save ham ends that you can buy for a reasonable price. Other luncheon meats can also be mixed in.

Chicken Salad

1 c. cooked and chopped chicken
¼ c. salad dressing
¼ c. chopped pickles (your favorite)

Mix all ingredients together. Serve on bread as a sandwich or on Ritz crackers.

Cooked Shrimp

1 ½ qt. boiling water
12 oz. shelled, deveined shrimp
1 clove garlic, crushed
1 tsp. creole or cajun seasoning
1 bay leaf

Bring water to a boil. Add seasonings and shrimp. Boil 1 minute or until pink and cooked through.

Cajun Sauce for Shrimp

1 Tbsp. sour cream

2 Tbsp. horseradish

¼ c. ketchup

2 Tbsp. creole or Dijon mustard

1 Tbsp. mayonnaise

½ tsp. creole seasoning

¼ tsp. hot pepper sauce

Mix all ingredients well, refrigerate.

Chicken Nuggets

1 whole chicken breast, skinnned and boned

2 Tbsp. vegetable oil

1 egg

1 Tbsp. water

3 Tbsp. flour

1 tsp. sesame seeds (optional)

¾ tsp. salt

Cut chicken in 1 inch pieces. Heat 1½" oil in iron skillet over medium heat until oil reaches 375°. Meanwhile, beat egg and water in bowl, add flour, sesame seeds and salt, stirring till batter is smooth. Dip chicken into batter, draining off excess. Fry chicken in hot oil about 4 minutes or until golden brown. Drain on paper towels. Serve with one of the sauces on the next page.

A false friend and a shadow attend when the sun shines. -BF

Pineapple Sauce

6 oz. pineapple, peach pineapple, or quince preserves.
2 Tbsp. mustard
2 Tbsp. horseradish

Combine in small saucepan. Cook and stir over low heat for 5 minutes.

Country Sauce

½ c. ketchup
3 Tbsp. butter
1 Tbsp. vinegar
1 tsp. brown sugar
¼ tsp. dry mustard

Combine in small saucepan. Cook and stir over low heat for 5 minutes.

Dill Sauce

¼ c. sour cream
¼ c. salad dressing
1 Tbsp. finely-chopped dill pickle
½ tsp. dill weed

Mix together in small bowl and cover. Refrigerate for 1 hour.

Alter the color of blue and pink hydrangeas
by adding acid to your soil.
Add aluminum sulfate for blue blooms,
and lime for pink blooms.

Bittersweet Chicken Wings

¼ c. flour

½ tsp. salt

⅛ tsp. pepper

12–16 chicken wings

4 Tbsp. butter, divided

2 Tbsp. lemon juice

1 Tbsp. orange peel

2 Tbsp. honey

1 tsp. soy sauce

Combine flour, salt and pepper in a plastic bowl with lid. Add wings; shake to coat completely with flour mixture. Melt 2 tablespoons butter in baking pan. Roll wings in butter to coat all sides. Arrange in single layer on pan. Bake for 30 minutes at 350°. Meanwhile, melt remaining 2 tablespoons butter in small saucepan. Stir in lemon juice, orange peel, honey and soy sauce. Remove wings from oven. Turn pieces over. Pour honey mixture over wings. Continue baking, basting occasionally, 30 minutes or until wings are tender.

Barbecue Chicken Wings

8–10 chicken wings

16 oz. tomato cocktail

2 tsp. minced onions

1 Tbsp. Worcestershire sauce

1 tsp. lemon pepper

2 Tbsp. brown sugar, heaping

2 Tbsp. barbecue sauce

1 Tbsp. honey

1 Tbsp. mustard

Mix together and pour over chicken wings in a casserole. Bake at 350° for 2 hours, uncovered, stirring occasionally. Just before serving, put wings on a cookie sheet and put in broiler for 3–5 minutes on each side. Leftover barbecue sauce can be refrigerated for another batch of wings later.

Barbecue Sauce for Ribs or Wings

½ c. ketchup

½ c. chopped onions

2 tsp. mustard

2 Tbsp. Worcestershire sauce

2 Tbsp. Southwest seasoning

¾ c. brown sugar

½ c. chopped hot peppers (I used home canned peppers)

1 tsp. garlic salt

¼ c. Jack Daniels whiskey

¼ c. honey

2 Tbsp. Chipotle tabasco sauce

½ c. vinegar

½ c. wine

Cook together until desired thickness.

Smoothie

1 ½ c. orange juice

1 banana, peeled

12 ice cubes

Blend on high until smooth and creamy.

Creamy Lime Chiller

1 c. milk

1 c. lime sherbet

¼ c. limeade concentrate

Place all ingredients in a blender, and process until smooth. Pour into chilled glasses and serve immediately.

Orange Sherbet Drink

1 pt. orange sherbet
2 cans 7-Up

Mix together until slushy. If too thick and slushy, add more 7-Up. Enjoy!

Breakfast Drink

2 oz. frozen orange juice concentrate
⅓ c. cold water
⅓ c. milk
1 Tbsp. sugar
⅓ tsp. vanilla
4 ice cubes

Combine first five ingredients in blender. Add 2 ice cubes at a time; process at high speed. Blend till smooth. Serve. You can also mix the first five ingredients and serve over ice cubes.

Rhubarb Punch

1 c. punch, frozen in an ice cube ice tray
1 can 7-Up or Sprite

Crush half of ice before putting into 2 tall glasses. Add the pop. Top with a mint sprig. Very refreshing drink. Rhubarb punch recipe is in the Canning and Freezing, section page 238.

     A Gardener's Work

"Oh, Adam was a gardener
And God who made him sees,
That half a proper gardener's work
Is done upon his knees." ♡

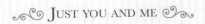

Lemonade

1 lg. lemon, squeezed

¼ c. sugar

1 c. water

1 c. crushed ice

Put all ingredients together in a glass with a tight fitting lid. Shake vigorously. Serve with a smile and a homemade cookie.

Strawberry Lemonade

1 pt. strawberries

2 tsp. sugar

8 Tbsp. sugar

8 Tbsp. lemon juice, freshly squeezed

soda water or seltzer

Purée strawberries and 2 teaspoons sugar in blender. Use two glasses; spoon 3 tablespoons strawberry purée, 4 tablespoons sugar and 4 tablespoons lemon juice into each glass. Stir the lemonade, add ice cubes. Top off with soda water. Add more sugar if needed.

Strawberry Daiquiri

2½ c. fresh or frozen strawberries

3 Tbsp. sugar

2 Tbsp. lime juice

3 c. ice cubes

Combine strawberries, sugar and lime juice in blender. Blend until smooth. Add ice cubes and blend until frothy. Serve in a tall, rimmed glass with sugar and lime slices.

Raspberry Sangria

1 lemon, sliced

2 limes, sliced

1 navel orange, peeled and sliced

1 doz. fresh raspberries

1 doz. fresh blueberries

1 doz. mint leaves, torn

2 c. ice cubes

1 bottle (non-alcoholic) sparkling red grape juice, chilled

In a large serving pitcher, combine the lemon, limes and orange. Add the raspberries, blueberries and mint. Add ice cubes. Pour chilled grape juice over fruit mixture and stir gently. It's delicious right away or let it set for several hours to allow the flavors to develop.

Rhubarb Iced Tea

4 stalks rhubarb (cut in 3" length)

4 c. water

sugar to taste

fresh mint sprigs

In a saucepan, combine rhubarb and water. Bring to a boil, and simmer for 1 hour. Strain off liquid, add sugar, stir until dissolved and cool. Serve over ice with a sprig of mint.

Place dips in edible bowls such as red, green and yellow pepper shells. *For fruit dips use melon,* orange or grapefruit shells.

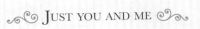

Friendship Tea

⅔ c. instant tea

2 pkg. dry lemonade mix

2 c. sugar

2 tsp. cinnamon

1¾ c. Tang

1 tsp. cinnamon

Mix all ingredients together. Store in a glass container. Use about 2 teaspoons mix to a cup of boiling water.

Hot Chocolate Mix

1 lb. powdered sugar

9.6 oz. box Carnation dry milk

8 oz. Nestles coffee creamer

8 oz. Nesquik chocolate flavor

Mix all together and store in a tight container. Three heaping teaspoons mix to a cup hot water. For a richer flavor, use milk. Top with minature marshmallows. This makes neat gifts. Fill empty peanut butter jars and add a bow or ribbon around the lid.

Cappuccino Mix

½ c. French vanilla coffee creamer

¾ c. hot chocolate mix

½ c. Carnation dry milk

½ c. powdered sugar

¼ c. sugar

¼ c. instant coffee, optional

Mix all together and put in an airtight container. To serve: Put 4 teaspoons (more or less to suit your taste) in a cup of hot water.

Homemade Hot Cocoa

¼ c. sugar

2 Tbsp. cocoa

dash of salt

2 Tbsp. hot water

2 c. milk

¼ tsp. vanilla

Combine sugar, cocoa and salt. Add hot water. Bring to a boil and simmer 2 minutes. Stir in milk. Heat to serving temperature. Do not boil.

Chocolate Syrup

½ c. cocoa

1 c. water

2 c. sugar

⅛ tsp. salt

¼ tsp. vanilla

Mix cocoa and water in a saucepan. Heat and stir until cocoa is dissolved. Add sugar, stir to dissolve. Boil 3 minutes. Add salt and vanilla. Pour into a pint jar. Store in refrigerator. Keeps for several months. This should be about half the price as Hershey's syrup. Everyone likes a glass of cold chocolate milk at Grandma's house.

When we grow old, I will take two chairs

and set them each in a sunlit day,

Then you and I in silent love, will rock the world away!

Cheese Ball

1 (8 oz.) cream cheese

1 c. shredded cheddar cheese

½ tsp. onion salt

1 tsp. Worcestershire sauce

½ tsp. lemon juice

¼ c. finely-chopped dried beef, optional

Form into a ball and roll in chopped walnuts. Serve with an assortment of crackers.

Creamy Cheese Ball

1 (8 oz.) cream cheese

4 oz. Velveeta cheese

1½ tsp. Worcestershire sauce

¼ tsp. onion salt

⅓ c. shredded cheddar cheese

½ tsp. chopped onion

Cream together cream cheese and Velveeta till well blended. Add remaining ingredients and mix well. Chill, then roll into a ball. Roll into chopped nuts or parsley flakes.

Vanilla Dip

1 (3.4 oz.) pkg. French vanilla or white chocolate instant pudding

1 c. milk

1 c. sour cream

1 tsp. vanilla

¼–½ tsp. almond extract

Whisk together pudding mix and milk until blended. Add next three ingredients and chill two hours. Serve with fruit. Yield: 2 cups.

Fruit Dip

1 (4 oz.) cream cheese

¼ c. sour cream

2 Tbsp. sugar

2 Tbsp. brown sugar

1–2 tsp. maple syrup or pancake syrup

Stir together and serve with fresh fruit.

Peanut Butter Dip

1 c. plain nonfat yogurt

½ c. powdered sugar

¼ c. creamy peanut butter

Mix together until smooth and serve with fruit. Yield: 1⅓ cups.

Pumpkin Dip

½ c. powdered sugar

1 oz. cream cheese

3 oz. pumpkin pie filling

¼ tsp. cinnamon

⅛ tsp. ginger

Combine all ingredients and mix well. Use dip with any kind of fresh fruit.

It doesn't take talent to be on time.

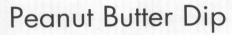

Fruit Dip

1 egg, beaten

¼ c. sugar

½ tsp. ReaLemon

½ tsp. McCormick orange peel

1 (4 oz.) cream cheese

4 oz. Cool Whip

Mix together egg, sugar, Realemon and orange peel; cook about one minute or until dissolved. When mixture is cold, add cream cheese and Cool Whip. Mix well. Serve with any fruit. Delicious!

Strawberry Yogurt Dip

1 (4 oz) cream cheese

½ c. sugar

8 oz. strawberry yogurt

4 oz. Cool Whip

Mix cream cheese and sugar together till well blended. Add yogurt; stir till smooth, then add Cool Whip. Serve with fresh fruit.

Hamburger Salsa Dip

1 lb. hamburger

1 c. salsa

Velveeta cheese

Fry hamburger. Drain if necessary. Add salsa and mix thoroughly. Add a few slices of Velveeta at a time, till desired taste. Stir until melted. This is good to take along to a coffee break. Reheat if necessary. Serve with Club or Ritz crackers or tortilla chips.

Chip Dip

1 (4 oz.) cream cheese

1 c. sour cream

½ c. salsa

finely-shredded cheddar cheese

Mix cream cheese and sour cream together till creamy. Spread evenly on a small plate or tray. Spread salsa evenly over first mixture. Sprinkle cheese over top. Finely-shredded lettuce can be added too. Serve with chips or pretzels. To make a fancy dish, set chip on end in salsa.

Onion Dip

1 lg. sweet onion

1 Tbsp. vegetable oil

½ tsp. dried thyme

½ c. mayonnaise

1 c. sour cream

¼ tsp. salt

⅛ tsp. pepper

Slice onion thinly, cut slices in half. Heat oil in a nonstick pan. Add onion and thyme; cover. Stir occasionally for 25 minutes or until golden brown. Remove cover. Cook 5 minutes. Cool. Add remaining ingredients after onions have cooled. Refrigerate one hour. Serve with raw vegetables.

Vegetable Dip

1 c. sour cream

½ pkg. Hidden Valley Ranch dressing mix

Mix together. Dip all kinds of vegetables in it, or your favorite potato chips.

Vegetable Dip

⅓ c. salad dressing

⅓ c. sour cream

½ tsp. onion powder

1 tsp. dill weed

Combine ingredients and mix well. Store in tight container in refrigerator. This can also be used on sandwiches.

Italian Vegetable Dip

½ c. Miracle Whip

¼ c. sour cream

½ env. Italian salad dressing mix of your choice

¼ c. finely-chopped green peppers

Mix all ingredients. Refrigerate. Serve with crackers or assorted cut up vegetables. Yield: 1 cup.

The greatest thing in the world is not so much where we are,

but in which direction we are moving.

Breakfast

Potato Cakes

1 ½ c. leftover mashed potatoes

2 eggs

4 Tbsp. flour

Mix all ingredients together till no lumps remain. Drop by tablespoonfuls on hot buttery griddle. Fry golden brown on both sides, flipping only once. Serve with gravy or maple syrup and canned peaches. Good for breakfast or dinner.

Berry Pancake

1 egg

¼ c. flour

¼ c. milk

1 Tbsp. butter

1 tsp. sugar

a pinch of salt

1 c. blueberries

½ c. sliced strawberries

½ c. raspberries (or frozen mixed fruit)

sugar to taste

Beat egg, four, milk, butter, sugar and salt until smooth. Pour batter into an 8" cast iron skillet. Bake at 425° for 15 minutes. Reduce heat to 350° and bake 10–15 minutes longer. Meanwhile, combine berries and sugar in a bowl. Let set for 5 minutes. Serve pancake on a plate or be creative and serve in hot skillet. Spoon berries on pancake and top with whipped cream.

Plan ahead...

Noah didn't wait until the rain came to start building the ark!

Pancakes

2 c. flour

1 egg

2 tsp. baking powder

1 c. milk

1 tsp. salt

¼ c. sugar

¼ c. shortening, melted

Mix all together. Pour onto hot, lightly greased griddle using ¼ cup batter for each pancake. Bake until pancakes are puffed and bubbly. Flip and bake until golden on both sides.

Fluffy Pancakes

1 c. flour

1 Tbsp. sugar

2 tsp. baking powder

½ tsp. salt

1 egg yolk

1 c. milk

1 Tbsp. butter, melted

1 egg white, stiffly beaten

Mix flour, sugar, baking powder and salt together. Add egg yolk, milk and melted butter. Beat until smooth. Fold in beaten egg white. On a hot, lightly greased griddle pour ½ cup pancake mix. Bake until puffy and bubbly. Flip and bake other side. Serve hot with fresh maple syrup or pancake syrup.

Baked Oatmeal

¼ c. butter, melted

⅓ c. brown sugar

1 egg, beaten

¼ tsp. salt

1 tsp. baking powder

½ c. milk

1½ c. oatmeal

cinnamon, optional

Cream butter, sugar and egg. Add rest of the ingredients. Mix well. Pour in a shallow pan and bake at 350° for 30 minutes. At 15 minutes fluff up with a spoon and finish baking. Serve with yogurt, fresh fruit or milk.

Meat and Potato Quiche

1 c. coarsely-chopped raw potatoes

1 Tbsp. vegetable oil

2 Tbsp. chopped onions

⅓ c. grated cheese

⅓ c. meat

⅓ c. evaporated milk

1 egg, beaten

salt and pepper to taste

Mix potatoes and vegetables oil. Press in a casserole dish and bake at 425° for 20 minutes or until brown. Remove from oven. Mix rest of the ingredients and pour on top of the hot crust. Return to oven and bake 30 minutes or until golden brown. (Cornflake crumbs and melted butter mixed together is good to put on top.)

Sausage Gravy

¼ lb. bulk sausage

¼ c. flour

2 c. milk

½ tsp. salt

dash of pepper

Fry sausage in iron skillet till brown. Drain off all fat except two tablespoons. Stir in flour. Cook, stirring constantly, until thick and bubbly. Gradually stir in milk, salt and pepper. If too thick, add more milk. Serve over homemade biscuits.

Barbecue Sausage

½ lb. sausage links or patties

1 tsp. butter

2 Tbsp. ketchup

1 tsp. mustard

1 tsp. brown sugar

¼ tsp. Worcestershire sauce

Brown sausage in butter. Combine remaining ingredients. Arrange sausage in small casserole. Brush sauce on each piece. Cover and bake at 350° for 45 minutes to 1 hour.

Bacon, Egg and Cheese Omelet

2 eggs, scrambled

3 slices Velveeta cheese

4 slices bacon

Scramble and fry eggs. Put cheese on half of fried eggs, add bacon. Fold other half of egg over cheese and bacon. Season with salt to taste. Serve immediately.

Omelet

1 Tbsp. butter
3 eggs, lightly beaten
salt and pepper to taste

Toppings:
shredded cheese
chopped ham
chopped peppers
chopped tomatoes
chopped onions
sliced mushrooms

Melt butter in a skillet over medium heat. Add eggs. Allow eggs to cook till set. Season with salt and pepper. Loosen omelet from pan. Place desired toppings on half of omelet. Fold in half. Turn onto serving plate.

Fried Rice

1 Tbsp. butter
1½ c. cooked rice
2 eggs, beaten

Melt butter in skillet, add rice and eggs. Stir constantly till eggs are fried. Serve with applesauce, or top with pancake syrup.

A good angle to approach any
problem is the try-angle.

Homemade Waffle Syrup

½ c. brown sugar

½ c. sugar

⅓ c. white Karo

2 Tbsp. water

½ tsp. maple flavoring

¼ tsp. butter flavoring

¼ tsp. vanilla

Cook till sugar is melted and syrup is the right consistency. Serve warm over waffles.

Coffee Soup

1 slice homemade bread

1 c. coffee, extra strong

1 tsp. brown sugar, maple syrup, cream or half-and-half

Break bread into bit-size pieces into your cereal bowl. Sprinkle with sugar to suit your taste. Add coffee and stir. Add cream to your desire. Serve with a hot dog sandwich. A traditional Sunday morning breakfast among the Amish families. Delicious!

To become perfect, follow the advice you give others.

Scrambled Eggs/Vanilla Sauce

4 eggs

Sauce:
¼ c. sugar
1 Tbsp. clear jel
1 tsp. flour
pinch of salt
1 egg yolk
1 c. milk
1 tsp. butter
¼ tsp. vanilla

In a saucepan combine sugar, clear jel, flour, salt, egg yolk and milk. Stir with whisk till well blended. Bring to a boil stirring constantly. Continue cooking till slightly thick. Set aside. Put 1 teaspoon butter in skillet, melt and add eggs. Fry and scramble till golden brown. Pour vanilla sauce over eggs. Serve with bacon, sausage links or fresh fruit. Note: Vanilla sauce is also good served over fresh fruit, hot or cold.

Life is a beautiful garden,
An ever-growing thing,
Where thoughtfulness
And kindness bloom
Like flowers in the spring.

Breakfast in a Loaf

4 c. all-purpose flour, divided

2 Tbsp. sugar

½ tsp. salt

2 Tbsp. yeast

1 c. water

¼ c. mustard

2 Tbsp. butter

½ c. chopped ham

¼ c. bacon bits

½ c. hash browns or Tater Tots, crumbled

scrambled eggs

1 c. shredded cheddar and mozzarella cheese

chopped pickles

Set aside 1 cup flour. Mix three cups flour, sugar, salt and yeast. Heat water, mustard and butter until melted. Stir into flour mixture. Mix thoroughly, add enough reserved flour to make a soft dough. Divide dough in half. Put on a greased 9"x13" cookie sheet as you would for pizza crust. Mix ham, bacon, eggs, potatoes, cheese and pickles together or layer down the middle of the pan. Make 1" cuts from outside edge of pan into the filling. Bring strips in from each side, twisting or braiding over filling. Let rise 15 minutes. Brush with beaten eggs. Repeat with second braid. Bake at 350° for 25 minutes or till golden brown. After baked and cold. Wrap and put in freezer for later. Thaw heat and serve. My version: I make sure I have plenty of ingredients for the filling. I like to pile them high, as long as you can still easily braid it. Make sure your filling is room temperature or warmer, but not hot. Make 6–8 braids and put in freezer for a quick and easy meal for yourself or unexpected company. Or you can take along to a friend's house for coffee break or brunch. To make only one braid use a 12"x17" pan.

Check in Meat & Main Dishes section for the Dinner in a Loaf.

Oatmeal for Breakfast

1 c. water

pinch of salt

drop of vanilla

¾ c. old fashioned rolled oats

brown sugar

In a saucepan bring water, salt and vanilla to a boil. Add oatmeal. Turn off heat. Press oatmeal down with a spoon so all is wet. Put cover on saucepan. Let set 10 minutes. Serve hot with a piece of chocolate cake and peaches. Add milk and brown sugar to your taste. Quick oats may be used instead. Note: Chocolate cake is good with brown sugar frosting.

Creamy Oatmeal

¾ c. old-fashioned rolled oats

1 ½ c. milk

¼ c. raisins

2 tsp. sugar

pinch of salt

Combine oats, milk, raisins, sugar and salt in saucepan over medium heat. Bring to a boil, stirring occasionally. Reduce heat and simmer five minutes. Cover, and remove from heat. Let stand five minutes.

Egg in a Hole

2 egg

2 pieces of bread

Melt butter in skillet. Meanwhile tear a 2" hole out of the center of a piece of bread. Put bread on skillet. Break egg into hole in bread. When bread is nicely toasted, add more butter and flip bread with egg in center. When egg is done and bread is toasted, flip onto plate. Put syrup on top. Cut off pieces of toast and dip in the egg (over easy.) Serve with fresh fruit.

Bacon, Egg, and Cheese Sandwich

2 pieces bread

1 egg

1 slice marble cheese

3 pieces bacon

Fry bacon; set aside. Scramble and fry egg. When egg is done, top with cheese. Put on a piece of bread with slices of bacon. Top with second piece of bread. Serve with fresh fruit or a glass of orange juice.

Ham and Eggs for Breakfast

½ c. cut-up ham

4 eggs

1 tsp. salt

⅓ c. milk

1 tsp. flour

Fry ham in skillet. Mix remaining ingredients well and add to ham. Fry till ready, stirring occasionally.

Save bacon drippings. Put in ½ pint jars. When cold put lid on and store in refrigerator. Use instead of margarine or butter when you fry potatoes. Potatoes will not stick to the bottom of your pan as much.

Breakfast Casserole

1 tube buttermilk biscuits
2 eggs, scrambled
Tater Tots or home fries
Velveeta Cheese
½ c. hamburger or sausage
3 Tbsp. butter
2 Tbsp. flour
1 c. milk
salt and pepper to taste

Place biscuits in a small greased casserole. Bake lightly, not brown. Remove from oven and let cool. Add a layer of Tater Tots and scrambled eggs, hamburger or sausage. Add gravy, Return to oven and heat thoroughly, about 15–20 minutes. Top with slices of Velveeta cheese. *Gravy*: Fry hamburger or sausage. Pour off grease. Add butter and flour. Stir constantly till nice and brown. Slowly add milk and continue stirring. If gravy is too thick, add more milk. Add salt and pepper to taste. This casserole can be prepared the day before.

Sausage Egg Casserole

¼ lb. sausage
2 eggs
⅓ c. milk
¼ tsp. dry mustard
¼ tsp. salt
1 slice bread, diced
¼ c. grated cheese

Brown sausage in skillet and drain. Beat eggs, milk, mustard and salt together. Add bread, cheese and sausage. Chill overnight. Bake at 350° for 45–50 minutes.

Southern Biscuits

⅓ c. shortening

1¾ c. flour

2½ tsp. baking powder

¾ tsp. salt

¾ c. milk

Mix flour, baking powder, shortening and salt until mixture resembles fine crumbs. Stir in just enough milk so dough leaves side of bowl and rounds into a ball. Turn dough onto lightly floured surface. Knead lightly. Roll one-half inch thick. Cut with biscuit cutter. Bake on ungreased cookie sheet at 450° for 10–12 minutes or till golden brown. Remove immediately from cookie sheet. You can also cut the dough with a donut cutter. Stretch and twist in a figure 8. Press so center sticks together. Dip in ½ cup melted butter, then in a mixture of 1 cup sugar and 1 teaspoon cinnamon. Bake same as biscuits.

Cheddar Garlic Biscuits

1 c. Bisquick

½ c. milk, scant

¼ c. shredded cheddar cheese

2 Tbsp. butter, melted

¼ tsp. garlic powder

Stir Bisquick, milk and cheese until soft ball forms. Drop by spoonfuls onto ungreased cookie sheet. Bake at 450° for 8–10 minutes or until golden brown. Stir together melted butter and garlic powder and brush over warm biscuits.

To talk without thinking is to shoot without aiming.

JUST YOU AND ME

It Only Takes A Moment

It only takes a moment
To whisper words of praise,
To thank God for all the blessings
That decorate your days.

It only takes a moment
To lift someone in prayer,
Who needs to be encouraged
And to know that God is always there.

It only takes a moment
To share a little love,
With someone who is lonely
And lift their soul above.

It only takes a moment
To be a friend in need,
And spread a little sunshine
While doing that good deed.

Life can be so complicated
Sometimes we forget to see,
That it only takes a moment
To be the best that we can be!

Breads, Rolls
Muffins & Cereals

Brown Bread

1 Tbsp. brown sugar

1 Tbsp. sugar

2 tsp. Thesco flour

¼ c. boiling water

½ c. cold water

1 Tbsp. yeast

pinch of salt

3 oz. Wesson oil

1 c. whole wheat flour

3 c. Thesco flour

Put first five ingredients in a bowl. Stir until sugar is dissolved. Add yeast and salt. Let set until yeast starts to rise. Add oil and flour and knead. Let rise. Knead every 15 minutes for 1 hour. Put in pan and let rise till double. Bake 25 minutes at 350°. Remove from pan and brush top with butter. Note: Instead of brushing tops with butter put bread in bags while still warm.

I have learned that to have a good friend

is the purest of all God's gifts,

for it is a love that has no exchange of payment.

Honey Wheat Bread

1½–1¾ c. Thesco flour

1 Tbsp. yeast

3 Tbsp. warm water

1 c. milk, scalded

3 Tbsp. honey

½ tsp. salt

3 Tbsp. vegetable oil

1 c. whole wheat flour

Put 1 cup Thesco flour in mixing bowl. Add yeast and warm water and mix well. Add scalded and cooled to lukewarm milk, honey, salt and oil to flour and yeast mixture. Add rest of flour, ⅓ cup at a time, mixing well each time. Knead till smooth and elastic. Place in greased bowl and let rise until double. Punch dough down and form into a loaf. Place in a greased pan. Cover and let rise until double. Bake 25–30 minutes at 350°. Brush top with melted butter. Remove from pan. If using pasteurized milk, heat to lukewarm.

Soft Gingerbread

¼ c. butter, softened

½ c. sugar, scant

1 egg

½ c. molasses

1⅓ c. flour

¾ tsp. baking soda

¼ tsp. salt

½ tsp. cinnamon

¼ tsp. ginger

⅛ tsp. cloves

½ c. hot water

Cream butter and sugar. Beat in egg and molasses. Add dry ingredients and beat till smooth. Blend in hot water. Pour in a greased 7"x9" pan. Bake at 325° for 35 minutes.

Country Bread

3 c. flour

1 tsp. salt

1 tsp. baking soda

2 Tbsp. honey

2 c. milk

1 c. raisins

Mix all ingredients until smooth. Fold in raisins. Pour into a greased loaf pan. Bake at 350° for 45 minutes. Cool before serving. Great for breakfast or an after school snack.

Banana Nut Bread

½ c. sugar

¼ c. butter

1 egg

2 bananas, mashed

1 c. flour

½ tsp. baking soda

pinch of salt

¼ c. nuts

Mix all ingredients together and pour into a loaf pan. Bake at 350° for 45 minutes or until done.

Take all bread out of pan and cool
before slicing for nicer slices.

Garlic Bread

2–3 slices homemade bread, cut in half

⅓ c. butter, melted

1 c. shredded mozzarella cheese

garlic salt

Melt butter and mix with cheese and garlic salt until well blended. Spread on surface of bread slices. Broil 2–3 minutes or until cheese mixture is bubbly. Serve with pizza or spaghetti or as an appetizer.

Apricot Nut Bread

1 c. chopped, dried apricots

1 c. water

1 egg

¾ c. sugar

2 Tbsp. butter, melted

¾ c. orange juice

2 c. flour

3 tsp. baking powder

¼ tsp. baking soda

½ tsp. salt

1 c. chopped walnuts

Soak apricots in water for a half hour. Drain. Mix egg, sugar and melted butter. Add orange juice and dry ingredients. Mix well and fold in apricots and chopped nuts. Bake in loaf pan at 350° for 1 hour. Remove from pan to cool.

Fruit Bread

1 (8 oz.) can crushed pineapple, drained, save juice
juice of 1 orange
¼–½ c. milk
1 Tbsp. grated orange peel
2 eggs
⅓ c. brown sugar
2 Tbsp. vegetable oil
2 Tbsp. poppy seeds, optional
2 c. flour
2 tsp. baking powder
½ tsp. salt

Combine juices; add enough milk to make a half cup. Add orange peel, eggs, sugar, vegetable oil and poppy seeds. Mix well and add flour, baking powder and salt. Fold together until blended. (Do not over mix.) Pour into a 9" greased loaf pan. Bake at 350° for 45–50 minutes.

It has been said that chickens will
cross a muddy road only one way,
because they don't want to be
dirty double crossers.

Zucchini Bread

3 eggs, beaten

2 c. sugar

1 c. vegetable oil

2 tsp. vanilla

1 tsp. salt

1 Tbsp. cinnamon

1 tsp. soda baking

1¼ tsp. baking powder

3 c. flour

1 c. chopped nuts

2 c. grated zucchini

Mix eggs, sugar and vegetable oil until well blended. Add vanilla, salt, cinnamon, soda, baking powder. Mix well and add flour and nuts. Fold in zucchini. Pour in two loaf pans. Bake at 325° for 1 hour. Serve warm with butter. Freeze 1 loaf for later. Optional: Chopped nuts or dates may be added.

Pizza Crust

1 c. warm water

1 Tbsp. yeast

2 Tbsp. sugar

2 Tbsp. vegetable oil

1 tsp. salt

2½ c. flour

Mix all ingredients together. Let stand 5 minutes. Press in pan. Top with your favorite toppings. Bake at 350° until crust is done.

Pizza Hut Crust

1½ tsp. yeast

2 tsp. sugar

½ c. warm water

2 tsp. vegetable oil

dash of garlic salt

¼ tsp. salt

1½ c. all-purpose flour

⅛ tsp. oregano

Mix first three ingredients. Let set five minutes, then add rest of ingredients. Mix all together, spread on a buttered 8"x13" pizza pan. Prick dough with fork. Let set 10 minutes. Bake 10 minutes at 350°. Meanwhile mix together your toppings: fried hamburger, peppers, onions, mushrooms, and 2 cups pizza sauce. Warm it in a saucepan, but not hot. Spread on crust, return to oven and finish baking until crust is golden brown. Approximately 15–20 minutes.

Pizza Dough

½ c. warm milk

¼ c. butter

¼ tsp. salt

2 Tbsp. sugar

2 tsp. yeast

1 egg, beaten

1½ c. flour, approximately

Melt butter in warm milk. Add yeast and rest of ingredients with flour last. Press into a greased 8"x13" pan, extending dough 1½" up the side. Let set 10 minutes. Add pizza sauce, your favorite toppings and cheese. Bake at 350° for 15 minutes or till done.

Pizza Dough

3 oz. warm water

1 tsp. yeast

1 ¼ c. Bisquick

Dissolve yeast in warm water and add Bisquick. Press in greased 8"x13" pan, with dough pressed up the sides about 1 ½". Let set 10 minutes. Put on your favorite toppings of fried hamburger, fried sausage, pepperoni etc. Top with sauce. Last sprinkle shredded cheese on top. Bake at 350° for 15 minutes or until edges of crust are tinted brown.

Breadsticks

½ c. flour

½ tsp. sugar

½ tsp. baking powder

pinch of garlic salt

¼ c. milk, scant

2 Tbsp. butter, melted

sesame seeds, optional

In a small bowl, combine flour, sugar, baking powder and salt. Gradually add milk and stir to form a soft dough. Turn onto a floured surface, knead gently 3–4 times. Roll into a rectangle; cut into 6 breadsticks. Place bread sticks in the butter and turn to coat. Sprinkle with seeds. Bake at 450° for 14–18 minutes or until golden brown. Serve warm.

It's a small world,
but I wouldn't want to paint it.

Butterhorns

1 ¾ c. flour

1 ½ Tbsp. sugar

½ c. butter

pinch of salt

½ c. milk, scalded, then cooled to lukewarm

2 eggs

1 ½ tsp. yeast

Mix first four ingredients until crumbly. Add milk to flour mixture. Add rest of ingredients. Roll out like pie crust. Cut in 4 pieces and roll up like crescent rolls. Chill a few hours or overnight. Roll out and add melted butter, brown sugar, cinnamon and nuts. Roll up again. Let set half an hour. Bake at 350° for 10 minutes. If using pasteurized milk, heat to lukewarm.

Cornbread

4 c. cornmeal

4 ¼ c. all-purpose flour

¾ c. sugar

¼ c. baking powder

1–2 tsp. salt

1 c. shortening

1 egg, beaten

1 c. milk

Mix all dry ingredients together. Cut in shortening until crumbly. This can be stored in 2⅓ cup portions in freezer in zip-lock freezer bags up to 6 months. To make the cornbread take 2⅓ cup cornmeal mixture and add; beaten egg and milk. Mixture will be lumpy. Bake at 425° for 20 minutes in a 9" iron skillet or heavy baking dish. Serve warm, smothered with butter.

Pluckets

1 (16 oz.) loaf frozen bread dough, cut in half

¼ c. chopped nuts

1 ½ oz. butterscotch pudding mix (cook and serve)

½ c. brown sugar

¼ c. butter

½ tsp. cinnamon

½ tsp. vanilla

¼ c. milk

Grease an 5"x8½" bread pan. Sprinkle nuts on bottom. In a saucepan combine pudding, sugar, butter, cinnamon, vanilla and milk. Bring to a boil and boil 3 minutes. Let cool, then pour a half cup pudding mixture over nuts. Cut bread dough into cubes and place on top of mixture. Pour remaining pudding mixture over dough. Cover with wax paper and refrigerate overnight. Bake uncovered on 350° for 30 minutes. Remove from oven and invert on plate. Also good for a morning coffee break. Note: Put other half of loaf in freezer for later use.

Caramel Buns

1 tube biscuits

¼ c. butter, lightly browned

⅓ c. brown sugar

¼ c. Karo or pancake syrup

chopped nuts

Combine butter, sugar and Karo. Heat till it starts to boil around edges. Add nuts. Put in bottom of loaf pan. Pull apart biscuits and put on top of sauce. Bake at 375° till done. Invert pan while hot. Eat while warm.

Feather Light Muffins

½ c. sugar
⅓ c. shortening
1 egg
½ c. milk
1½ tsp. baking powder
½ tsp. salt
¼ tsp. nutmeg
1½ c. flour

Topping:
½ c. sugar
1 tsp. cinnamon
½ c. butter, melted

Cream sugar, shortening and egg. Add dry ingredients to creamed mixture alternately with milk. Fill muffin pans ⅔ full. Bake at 325° for 15–20 minutes or until done. Dip top of muffins in melted butter, then in cinnamon and sugar mixture. 8–10 muffins. These are nice to make in the mini muffin pans for a backyard coffee break. Serve warm.

Keep your fears to yourself, but share your courage with others.

Ham and Cheese Muffins

1 c. flour
1 ¼ tsp. baking powder
¼ tsp. salt
¼ tsp. paprika
¼ c. grated cheese
¼ c. chopped ham
1 egg
½ c. milk
2 Tbsp. shortening, melted

Mix flour, baking powder, salt, paprika, cheese and ham in a bowl. In a separate bowl, beat egg; add milk and melted shortening. Combine mixture, stirring enough to moisten. Fill muffin cups ⅔ full. Bake at 400° for 20–25 minutes. Yield: 6 muffins.

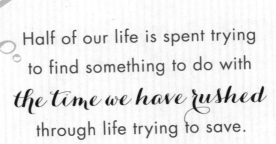

Half of our life is spent trying
to find something to do with
the time we have rushed
through life trying to save.

Hearty Muffins

1¼ c. flour

½ c. sugar

1 tsp. baking powder

1 tsp. baking soda

1 tsp. cinnamon

½ tsp. nutmeg

pinch of salt

1 egg, beaten

¼ c. vegetable oil

1 c. chopped apples

½ c. shredded carrots

½ c. dried cranberries

½ c. chopped nuts

In a bowl, combine flour, sugar, baking powder, baking soda, cinnamon, nutmeg and salt. In a separate bowl, mix eggs and oil; add apples, carrots, cranberries and nuts. Mix with dry ingredients. Batter will be thick. Fill muffin pan ¾ full. Bake at 350° for 20–25 minutes or till done. Yield: Approximately 12 muffins.

If you really want to be happy
nobody can stop you.

Banana Muffins

½ c. flour

¼ c. whole wheat flour

1 tsp. baking powder

dash of salt

1 egg, beaten

¼ c. honey

¼ c. mashed banana

3 Tbsp. milk

2 Tbsp. vegetable oil

½ tsp. orange peel

¼ c. chopped nuts

Place cupcake papers in pans. Set aside. Combine flours, baking powder and salt. Make a well in center. Combine egg, honey, banana, milk, oil and orange peel in another bowl. Add all at once to dry mixture. Stir just until moistened. Stir in nuts. Spoon batter in muffin pan. ¾ full. Bake at 400° for 10–12 minutes.

Blueberry Muffins

1¾ c. flour

¼ c. sugar

2½ tsp. baking powder

¾ tsp. salt

1 egg, beaten

⅓ c. vegetable oil or ¾ c. milk

1 c. blueberries

Stir together flour, sugar, baking powder and salt. Combine egg, milk and vegetable oil. Make a hole in center of dry ingredients. Add egg mixture; stir quickly, just till dry ingredients are moistened. Stir in blueberries. Fill muffin pan ⅔ full. Bake at 400° for 25 minutes. Yield: 12 muffins.

Nutty Fruit-Filled Muffins

2 c. flour
½ c. sugar
1 Tbsp. baking powder
½ tsp. cinnamon
½ tsp. salt
2 eggs
½ c. milk
½ c. butter, melted
jam

Prepare Streusel Topping below and set aside. In a large bowl, mix flour, sugar, baking powder, cinnamon and salt. In a small bowl, beat eggs with fork. Stir in milk and butter. Add to flour mixture; stir just until blended. For muffins, fill greased pans about ⅓ full; top with jam. Add more batter to fill cups about ⅔ full. Sprinkle with Streusel Topping. Bake in preheated 400° oven for 15–20 minutes or until toothpick inserted in center comes out clean.

Streusel Topping

¼ c. chopped walnuts
3 Tbsp. flour
3 Tbsp. sugar
3 Tbsp. butter, melted
¼ tsp. nutmeg

Mix all ingredients until crumbly.

Apple, Cinnamon Muffins

⅔ c. flour, scant

⅓ c. apple cinnamon flavored Malt-O-Meal hot cereal, dry

¼ c. sugar

⅓ c. milk

2 Tbsp. vegetable oil

1 egg

1 tsp. baking powder

¼ tsp. salt

Mix all ingredients together till well moistened. Fill greased muffin pans ¾ full. Bake at 400° for 15 minutes or when center is firm to the touch. Hint: for moister muffins, add ¼ cup applesauce. Yield: 6 muffins.

Soft Pretzels

1 tsp. dry yeast

¾ c. warm water

½ Tbsp. sugar

½ tsp. salt

2 c. flour

1 egg, beaten

salt to taste

Dissolve yeast in warm water. Add sugar, salt and flour; mix well. Knead till smooth. Divide into 12 portions. Twist into pretzel shapes. Place on greased cookie sheets. Brush with beaten egg and sprinkle with salt. Bake at 400° for 12–15 minutes, or until light brown. Serve warm. Yield: 12 pretzels.

Grape Nuts

2½ c. brown sugar

4 c. whole wheat flour

1 tsp. vanilla

½ tsp. salt

¾ c. butter, melted

½ tsp. baking soda

Mix all ingredients together. Bake at 350°. When done crumble up cake. Put in pans and bake till golden brown. Stir occasionally while baking.

Peanut Butter Granola

5 c. oatmeal

1 c. wheat germ

½ c. coconut

¾ c. brown sugar

1 pkg. graham crackers, crushed

⅓ c. butter

⅓ c. honey

1 tsp. vanilla

⅓ c. peanut butter

Mix all ingredients together in a mixing bowl. Place on cookie sheets and toast at 250° till golden brown. Stir occasionally.

Patience is the ability to idle *your motor when you feel* like stripping your gears.

Granola

5 c. rolled oats

½ c. sugar

½ c. brown sugar

½ c. toasted wheat germ

¾ c. coconut

1 c. sliced almonds, optional

¾ c. butter

Mix all ingredients in a large bowl except butter. Melt butter and pour over top and mix well. Place on cookie sheets and toast at 300° till golden brown. Also good with fresh fruit, ice cream or yogurt.

Marshmallow Topping

1 c. sugar

1 ¼ c. Karo

¼ c. water

½ c. Karo

3 egg whites, beat till stiff

Cook first three ingredients to 240°. Meanwhile in a bowl beat ½ c. Karo and egg whites until stiff peaks form. Add cooked mixture very slowly to egg whites with someone beating all the while. Scrape sides of bowl often. After cooked mixture is added, beat another 5 minutes. Stir occasionally until cold. If you're in a hurry, set bowl in cold water. Stir until cold. Put in jars immediately. Yield: 5 half pint jars. Can be used on top of hot chocolate or mixed with peanut butter or ½ cup strawberry freezer jam to spread on bread.

Peanut Butter Spread

¼ c. brown sugar

2 Tbsp. Karo

¾ c. water

1 c. peanut butter

2 c. marshmallow creme

Cook first three ingredients together until it comes to a rolling boil. Pour into a stainless steel bowl and cool. Add peanut butter. Mix until smooth. Add marshmallow topping and mix until smooth. This is good on a piece of fresh homemade bread, with a cup of coffee.

Peanut Butter Spread

2 c. maple flavored pancake syrup

1 c. peanut butter

½ c. marshmallow creme

Mix all ingredients together well. Store in tight container. Spread on homemade bread or toast. Yum!

When love and skill work
together, expect a masterpiece.

Herb Butter

½ c. butter, softened
1 clove of garlic, minced
1 tsp. parsley flakes
½ tsp. basil
½ tsp. thyme
garlic salt

Combine ingredients in a small bowl. Mix well. Pack in a small crock or a baby food jar with a decorative lid. Or roll into a log, place wax paper and twist ends. Chill thoroughly. Note: When wrapped in colorful paper, it makes a neat little gift, along with a loaf of bread for that friend that has everything. Yield: ½ cup.

Toasted Bread Crumbs for Dressing

Take a loaf of bread and slice and cut into ¾" cubes. Put one loaf bread on a large baking sheet; sprinkle with seasonings, (onion salt, garlic salt, Lawry's, etc.) Melt ½ cup butter and pour over top. Toast at 350° in oven, stirring occasionally. Toast until desired brownness. Can be used on salads too. Grandchildren like it for a snack. Store in glass jars to keep the flavor better. Dressing recipe is in Canning and Freezing section.

Do not follow where a path may lead,
go instead where there is no
path and leave a trail.

The Old Wooden Ice Box

I remember the old ice box,
I'm glad its days are past.
No matter how hard you tried,
The ice just would not last.

Every time the iceman came,
He had water all over the floor.
He'd chip the ice to make it fit,
Then he walked through the water to the door.

The pan underneath was always full,
You must dump it twice a day.
If you wanted ice for a cold drink,
You took the ice pick, and chipped away.

It seemed the floor was always wet,
There was water everywhere.
You mopped it up a dozen times,
But it seemed water was always there.

I'm glad those days are over,
I like the modern days you see.
My gas refrigerator is clean and neat,
It saves a lot of work for me.

Soups, Salads & Salad Dressings

Chicken Noodle Soup

2 c. chicken broth

¾ c. noodles

2 tsp. flour

¼ c. cold water

¾ c. chicken, cooked and diced

1 oz. heavy cream

salt and pepper to taste

parsley flakes, optional

Bring broth to a boil, add dry noodles. Cover and let stand 10 minutes. Meanwhile mix flour with water; stir till no lumps remain. Bring to a boil again, stirring constantly; add flour and water mixture. Stir till smooth; add chicken, cream, salt and pepper. Cover till ready to serve. Sprinkle with parsley flakes.

Old Fashioned Bean Soup

3 Tbsp. butter

2 c. milk

3 slices homemade bread

2 hard-boiled eggs

salt and pepper to taste

½ c. navy beans, smothered in brown butter

Brown butter in saucepan, add milk. Meanwhile cube the bread. When milk is hot, add cubed bread. Do not boil. When soup is in serving bowls top with sliced hard-boiled egg and beans. Buy a can of navy beans, or make your own. See recipes in Canning and Freezing section. Sweet pickles or pickled red beets on the side.

Quick Beef Soup

1 c. fried hamburger

½ c. chopped onions

1 tsp. garlic salt

1 c. tomato cocktail, home-canned

2 c. water

2 beef bouillon cubes

pinch of pepper

½ c. frozen mixed vegetables

Fry hamburger, onions, salt and pepper in saucepan until hamburger is brown. Drain fat. Add tomato cocktail, water and bouillon cubes to the meat mixture. Bring to a boil, reduce to simmer. Simmer uncovered 20 minutes. Add vegetables. Simmer 15 minutes more. Serve with garlic bread.

Potato Soup

1½ c. potatoes, washed and cubed

1¾ c. milk

3 Tbsp. flour

1 tsp. sugar

salt and pepper to taste

Combine all ingredients and bring to a boil. Stir constantly until thick. Let set 5 minutes before serving. If too thick, add a little more milk.

God has given us two hands,
one to receive with and the other to give with.

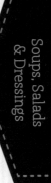

Chili Soup

4 c. tomato cocktail

2 c. fried hamburger

1 Tbsp. chopped onions

2 Tbsp. chili seasoning

3 Tbsp. taco sauce

1 Tbsp. Worcestershire sauce

¼ c. brown sugar

salt and pepper to taste

Put all together in saucepan and heat, but do not boil. Recipe for tomato cocktail sauce and fried hamburger can be found in Canning and Freezing section.

Fresh Fruit Soup

1 piece of bread (homemade or Italian)

½ c. fresh fruit, chopped and sweetened

½ c. milk

brown or white sugar to suit your taste

Tear bread in pieces into your cereal bowl. Pour fresh fruit and milk on top of your bread. Add sugar to suit your taste. Fresh strawberries, peaches, or sliced bananas is my choice. Serve with a hot dog or ham and cheese sandwich. A quick and easy meal on a hot summer evening.

A mother's arms are made of tenderness.

Apple Salad

⅓ c. cherry Jell-O

2 c. boiling water

1 apple, peeled, cored and chopped

chopped nuts, optional

Put Jell-O in bowl, add boiling water. Stir until dissolved. Let stand till almost set. Add chopped apple. Put in small glass bowl or Jell-O mold. Refrigerate till set. Top with whipped cream just before serving. Note: Use orange Jell-O and finely-shredded carrots. You can also put in a 6"x6" pan. When set, cut in four squares; serve on lettuce leaf with cottage cheese.

Refreshing Orange Salad

⅓ c. box orange Jell-O

¼ c. sugar

1½ c. boiling water

1 sm. can crushed pineapple

1 medium orange, peeled and chopped

Cool Whip

Prepare Jell-O and sugar with boiling water. Stir until dissolved. Add pineapple and oranges along with the juices. Set in refrigerator. Stir occasionally until it starts to set. Pour in a dish. Refrigerate until ready to serve. Top with Cool Whip when ready to serve.

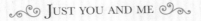

Orange Salad

⅓ c. orange Jell-O

2 c. boiling water

2 medium oranges, peeled

Put Jell-O and boiling water in a bowl. Stir until completely dissolved. Set aside until cold and slightly set. Take oranges and slice thin. Mix into Jell-O. Put in a clear glass bowl. Chill until set. Serve with cottage cheese or whipped cream. You can also put in a 6"x6" pan. Cut in 4 squares and serve on lettuce and cottage cheese.

Pear Salad

⅓ c. lime Jell-O

2 c. boiling water

4 pear halves, drained

Put Jell-O and boiling water in a bowl. Stir until completely dissolved. Let set until cold. Arrange pears in a 6"x6" pan, cut side down. Pour Jell-O over pears. If they want to float, prick with a fork so Jell-O can soak through. Chill until completely set. Cut so you have a pear in each square and serve on lettuce and cottage cheese, or top with whipped cream. Pears can be chopped before adding Jell-O. Then put in a clear glass bowl. Top with cottage cheese or topping just before serving.

Cranberry Salad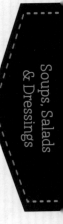

⅓ c. red Jell-O
½ c. boiling water
½ c. cold water
1½ c. cranberries
1 sm. orange
2 sm. apples
½ c. crushed pineapple
⅔ c. sugar
chopped walnuts, optional

Mix first two ingredients. Stir until dissolved, add cold water. Set aside. Grind or chop cranberries, oranges and apples. Mix with crushed pineapple and sugar. Mix all together. Refrigerate; stir occasionally until slightly set. Pour into a mold or a clear cut glass bowl or put in half cup containers so you don't take more out of refrigerator than you want to serve. Delicious!

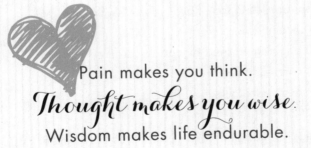

Pain makes you think.
Thought makes you wise.
Wisdom makes life endurable.

Cranberry Delight

1 (10 oz) crushed pineapple, drained, reserve juice
½ c. water
⅓ c. strawberry Jell-O
8 oz. whole berry cranberry sauce
4 tsp. lemon juice
½ tsp. grated lemon peel
¼ tsp. nutmeg
1 c. sour cream
¼ c. walnuts, chopped
fresh strawberries, optional

Combine pineapple juice and water; heat to boiling. Remove from heat, add Jell-O, stir until dissolved. Stir in cranberry sauce, lemon juice, peel and nutmeg. Chill until slightly thickened. Add sour cream and mix well. Fold in pineapples and nuts. Pour in mold. Chill until firm. Serve on a bed of lettuce decorated with strawberries and nuts.

Cottage Cheese and Pineapple Salad

1 c. cottage cheese
3 Tbsp. dry Jell-O, any flavor
½ c. coconut
1 (10 oz.) can crushed pineapple, drained
1 sm. can mandarin oranges, drained
½ c. sm. marshmallows
4 oz. Cool Whip

Mix together all ingredients, with cool whip folded in last.

Waldorf Salad

⅓ c. lemon Jell-O

1 c. boiling water

1 c. cold water

1 Tbsp. vinegar

1 c. diced apples

½ c. chopped celery

¼ c. chopped walnuts

Dissolve Jell-O in boiling water. Add cold water and vinegar. Chill until slightly thickened. Add remaining ingredients. Put in a serving bowl or in a pan. When set, cut in squares and add a dab of topping to serve.

Cream Cheese Salad

⅓ c. lime Jell-O

2 c. boiling water

1 (8 oz.) cream cheese

1 c. whipping cream

1 c. crushed pineapple

1 c. chopped celery

½ c. chopped nuts

Dissolve Jell-O in boiling water. Let stand until it begins to thicken. Whip cream cheese and whipping cream together. Whip into the Jell-O. Add pineapple, celery and nuts. Refrigerate until set in a glass bowl.

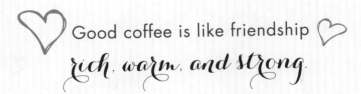

Good coffee is like friendship

rich, warm, and strong.

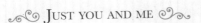

Cole Slaw

2 c. shredded cabbage

1 sm. carrot, shredded, optional

½ c. Miracle Whip

1 Tbsp. sugar

½ tsp. salt

½ c. milk

½ tsp. mustard

finely-chopped celery, optional

Shred cabbage and carrot. Put in bowl and set aside. Mix dressing ingredients together. Pour over cabbage and carrot mixture. Refrigerate till ready to serve.

German Slaw

1 sm. head of cabbage, shredded

1 sm. green pepper, chopped in small pieces

1 sm. red onion, sliced into rings

1 c. sugar

1 c. vinegar

1 c. vegetable oil

1 tsp. salt

1 Tbsp. celery seed

Combine cabbage, pepper and onion. Set aside. In small saucepan, mix sugar vinegar, oil, salt and celery seed. Bring to a boil, stirring until sugar is dissolved. Pour over slaw and chill until serving time.

Macaroni Salad

2 c. water

¾ c. macaroni

¼ c. Miracle Whip

⅓ c. milk

2 Tbsp. sugar

1 Tbsp. vinegar

½ tsp. salt

1 tsp. mustard

½ tsp. celery seed, optional

½ tsp. mustard seed, optional

¼ c. chopped celery, optional

¼ c. chopped carrots, optional

Bring water to a boil; add macaroni, and stir. Cover, turn off heat and let set 10 minutes. Drain, rinse immediately in cold water till macaroni is cold. Bring half cup water to a boil. Add chopped carrots. Cover, turn off heat and let set five minutes. Repeat draining process. Put macaroni, celery and carrots in bowl. Mix rest of ingredients together. Pour over mixture in bowl. Refrigerate 3 hours or make one day ahead.

Bacon Potato Salad

1 c. potatoes, cooked and cubed

6 slices fried bacon, crumbled

2 Tbsp. chopped green peppers

2 Tbsp. chopped onions

¼ c. Miracle Whip

salt and pepper if desired

Mix potatoes, bacon, green pepper and onions in bowl. Add Miracle Whip; mix lightly. Season with salt and pepper. Refrigerate.

Potato Salad

2 c. diced potatoes
1 sm. carrot, diced
1 stalk celery, diced
1 tsp. minced onions
1 hard-boiled egg, peeled and chopped

Dressing:
¾ c. Miracle Whip
1 tsp. vinegar
1 tsp. mustard
1 tsp. Worcestershire sauce
3 Tbsp. sugar
dash of salt
¼ tsp. dill weed
6 Tbsp. milk

Cook potatoes till slightly tender. Cool immediately in cold water. Drain. Mix first five ingredients together. Mix dressing and pour over vegetables; mix well. Refrigerate until ready to serve. If too thick, add a little more milk. If you want a tangier taste, add more vinegar, mustard and Worcestershire sauce.

There's nothing wrong with
underachieving,
it just doesn't pay very well.

Tossed Salad Dressing

3 c. Miracle Whip

2 c. sugar

1 tsp. salt

1 Tbsp. mustard

¼ c. vinegar

½ c. milk

1 tsp. celery seed

Mix all ingredients together. Stir until sugar is dissolved. Put in a glass jar in refrigerator. This dressing is a good keeper. If too thick, add a little more milk. I use this for Macaroni Salad and Potato Salad.

Dressing for Spinach Salad

¼ c. sugar

2 Tbsp. sesame seeds

1 ½ tsp. minced onions

¼ tsp. Worcestershire sauce

¼ tsp. paprika

½ c. vegetable oil

¼ c. vinegar

lettuce of your choice

spinach, torn into bite-sized pieces

sliced strawberries

chopped walnuts

mozzarella cheese

Put first seven ingredients in blender or gravy shaker and mix until well blended. Best when served cold.

French Dressing

½ c. ketchup
½ c. vegetable oil
2 Tbsp. vinegar
2 Tbsp. sugar
1 Tbsp. chopped onions
2 Tbsp. lemon juice
1 tsp. paprika

Put all ingredients in a shaker or blender. Shake until well blended. Refrigerate until ready to serve.

French Dressing

¼ c. vegetable oil
¼ c. sugar
¼ c. vinegar
¼ c. ketchup
¼ tsp. Worcestershire sauce
¼ tsp. salt

Beat all ingredients till well mixed. Yield: 1 cup.

Italian Dressing

½ c. vegetable oil

2 Tbsp. vinegar

⅛ tsp. garlic powder

¼ tsp. sugar

1 Tbsp. chopped onions

½ tsp. mustard

½ tsp. basil

¼ tsp. oregano

Put all ingredients in a shaker or blender. Shake until smooth and well blended. Refrigerate until ready to serve.

Grandma's Velvet Salad Dressing

½ c. sugar

2 Tbsp. flour

1 egg, beaten

2 Tbsp. vinegar

1 tsp. mustard

1 tsp. salt

1 c. cold water

Cook in saucepan, stirring constantly, until thick. Stir in three tablespoons butter. This may be mixed with whipped cream. Extra salt, sugar, or vinegar may be added to your taste. Use for potato salad or lettuce salad.

Croutons

bread

1 tsp. parsley flakes

¼ tsp. onion salt

¼ tsp. garlic salt

¼ c. butter

Cut about a half loaf of bread into cubes. Melt butter and stir in salts and parsley flakes. Put bread in a mixing bowl and add butter mixture. Toss around until bread is well coated. Put on cookie sheet and bake at 350° until desired crispness. Cool completely. Store in tight containers until ready to use on salads or vegetables, etc. More or less salts to suit your taste.

Egg Boats

3 hard-boiled eggs

1 Tbsp. Miracle Whip

¼ tsp. sugar

¼ tsp. mustard

pinch of salt

¼ tsp. vinegar

6 sm. cheese wedges, optional

paprika, optional

Put eggs in cold water; bring to a boil. Boil five minutes. Water must cover eggs. Put eggs in cold water to cool. Peel eggs and cut lengthwise. Take out yolks. Mash yolks with fork and add remaining ingredients, except cheese. Mix well. Spoon yolk mixture back in egg whites. Put cheese wedge on toothpick and stick in each boat. Sprinkle eggs with paprika. Yield: 6 boats.

JUST YOU AND ME

Meats
& Main Dishes

Pork & Beans

1 (11 oz.) can Bush pork & beans

2 Tbsp. brown sugar, heaping

½ tsp. Worcestershire sauce

½ tsp. mustard

1 tsp. barbecue sauce

2–3 hot dogs, sliced or ½ lb. hamburger

2 Tbsp. ketchup

1 sm. onion or minced onions

½ c. kidney beans, optional

½ c. lima beans, optional

½ c. green beans, optional

Drain all liquid off pork & beans. Pour beans in small casserole. Add all ingredients and heat at 300° until hot and bubbly. If you add kidney, lima and green beans you end up with a dish of baked beans. Add more or less of the spices to suit your taste.

As the earth can produce
nothing unless it is fertilized
by the sun, so we can do nothing
without the grace of God.

Oven Baked Beans

2 c. dry navy beans

8 c. cold water

1 tsp. salt, divided

⅔ c. brown sugar

1 tsp. dry mustard

½ c. dark molasses

¼ tsp. pepper

¼ lb. salt pork, cut up

½ c. finely-chopped onions

½ c. chopped celery

½ c. finely-chopped green peppers

Rinse beans; place in a Dutch oven with cold water. Bring to a boil; reduce heat and simmer for two minutes. Remove from heat; cover and let set for 1 hour. (Or omit boiling and soak beans in water overnight.) Add ½ teaspoon salt to beans and soaking water. Bring to a boil. Reduce heat, simmer covered for 1 hour. Drain, remove liquid. Combine brown sugar, mustard, molasses, pepper and remaining salt. Stir in 2 cups reserved cooking liquid. Add to beans with salt pork, onions, celery and green peppers. Put in a 2½ quart casserole. Cover and bake at 300° for 2½ hours. Stir occasionally or until beans are as thick as desired. Add more cooking liquid if necessary. Stir with a wooden spoon like Grandma did. Every time you open the oven door, the aroma seems richer and richer. These beans are delicious the second time around.

If at first you don't succeed,
then skydiving is not the hobby for you!

Depression Casserole

½ c. chopped onions

1–2 Tbsp. vegetable oil

½ c. ketchup

½ c. water

¼ c. vinegar

1 tsp. mustard

¼ tsp. pepper

1 lb. hot dogs, sliced thin

rice, toasted or cooked, optional

In a saucepan, sauté onion in oil until tender. Stir in ketchup, water, vinegar, mustard and pepper. Bring to a boil, stirring occasionally. Put hot dogs in a one-quart baking dish. Pour sauce over hot dogs. Bake uncovered at 375° for 30 minutes or until bubbly. Serve over toast or cooked rice. When the money is all gone and payday is several days away, this is still a satisfying meal.

Save leftovers and create a dish of
your own. Sometimes leftovers have
a better flavor than the first day. Add
slices of Velveeta cheese or add Tater
Tots. Heat in the oven until cheese is
melted, or heated thoroughly.

Dinner in a Loaf

1 c. water

¼ c. mustard

2 Tbsp. butter

4 c. all-purpose flour, divided

2 Tbsp. sugar

½ tsp. salt

2 Tbsp. yeast

1 c. shredded cheddar cheese

½ c. chopped pickles

1 egg, beaten

Heat water, mustard and butter until melted. Stir in 3 cups flour, sugar, salt and yeast. Mix thoroughly. Add enough reserve flour to make a soft dough. Knead four minutes. Divide dough in half. Put on a greased 9"x13" cookie sheet as you would for pizza crusts. Mix ham, cheese, etc. together or spread in layers down the middle of your pan. Make 1" cuts from outside edge of pan in to the filling. Bring strips in from each side to twist or braid over the filling. Let rise 15 minutes. Brush with beaten egg. Bake at 350° for 25 minutes or until golden brown. Repeat with second braid. After baked and cold, wrap in Saran Wrap. Put in freezer for later. Then thaw, heat and serve. My version: Fried hamburger, onions, peppers, bacon, ham, shredded Swiss cheese, pizza sauce. Mix everything together in a bowl. You have pizza flavor all the way through. I like to pile it high, as long as you can still easily braid it. Make sure filling is room temperature. To make only one use 12"x17" pan. Check in breakfast section for the Breakfast Braid Loaf.

Velveeta cheese boxes make
great drawer organizers.

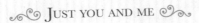

Potluck Potatoes

3 c. shredded potatoes
1 Tbsp. butter
¼ c. Velveeta cheese
¼ c. cream of mushroom soup
¼ c. sour cream
½– ¾ c. ham, cubed, optional

Topping:
¾ c. crushed cornflakes
1 Tbsp. butter, melted

Cook shredded potatoes in salt water until tender yet firm. Meanwhile melt together butter, Velveeta cheese and mushroom soup over low heat. Do not let it boil. Remove from heat and add sour cream. Drain potatoes and let set till they are cold before mixing with rest of ingredients. Add ham, salt and pepper to taste. Put in casserole and bake at 350° for 30 minutes. Add cornflakes and bake for another 10 minutes. Can be made a day ahead, potatoes must be cold before adding other ingredients. Refrigerate leftovers immediately.

Pan Fried Potatoes

2 c. potatoes, sliced or shredded
2 slices of onion or 1 tsp. minced onions
3 Tbsp. bacon drippings or butter

Wash and shred unpeeled potatoes. Fry in iron skillet till tender and golden brown. When ready to serve top with tomato gravy.

Fried Potatoes

2 leftover baked potatoes, sliced

8 slices bacon

1 sm. onion, sliced and chopped

Fry bacon in skillet, remove bacon when done. Fry potato and onion in bacon grease. Salt to taste. When done, sprinkle crumbled bacon over top. Serve with applesauce.

Baked Potatoes

2 baking potatoes

2 Tbsp. butter, melted

salt

Lawry's seasoned salt

Grease cookie sheet or large pie pan with vegetable oil. Cut potatoes lengthwise. Brush cut side with butter. Sprinkle with salts. Place in pan, salted side down. Bake at 350° for 30 minutes or until potatoes are tender when pricked with a fork. Serve with sour cream.

When buying ham,
about 3 servings per pound of bone-in ham,
4 servings per pound of boneless ham.

Toppings for Baked Potatoes

California Blend vegetables

fried hamburger or sloppy joe

chopped onions

chopped green and red peppers

fried bacon, crumbled

1 can cheddar cheese soup

1 can nacho cheese soup

sour cream

Steam frozen California Blend vegetables until tender. Drain. Chop finely with food chopper. Combine soups with one can milk. Heat until cheese is melted and hot. Don't boil. Add toppings onto your baked potato in any order. Add cheese sauce and last a big dab of sour cream. It's a meal by itself, or serve with a salad of your choice. Vegetables can be chopped ahead of time. Leftover cheese sauce will keep several days in refrigerator. Cheese sauce is also good on other vegetable dishes.

Creamy Lettuce for Potatoes

1 c. lettuce, torn up

¼ c. Miracle Whip

1 Tbsp. sugar

1 tsp. vinegar

2 Tbsp. milk

pinch of salt

2 med. potatoes, cubed and cooked in salt water

Mix Miracle Whip, sugar, vinegar, milk and salt. Pour over lettuce and mix well. Drain water off potatoes. Spoon lettuce over cubed or mashed potatoes.

Sour Cream for Baked Potatoes

1 ½ c. sour cream
1 Tbsp. light cream
¾ tsp. lemon juice
¼ tsp. garlic salt

Beat first two ingredients till light and fluffy. Add lemon juice and garlic salt. Blend well. Serve over potatoes or fried vegetables.

Mashed Potatoes (to make ahead)

1 ½ lb. potatoes
4 oz. cream cheese
4 Tbsp. butter
¼ c. sour cream
1 egg
¼ c. milk
½ tsp. salt

Peel and cook potatoes until tender. Drain off the water and mash the hot potatoes. Add cream cheese and butter. Beat well; add sour cream. Beat eggs, milk and salt together and add to potatoes. Mix well. Put in a one-quart casserole. Cover and refrigerate overnight. Bake at 350° for 45 minutes.

Dare to be the pack rat of the family, if you don't mind being laughed at. You will be the one who sells the most at your next family garage sale.

Or . . . a family member will come and ask, "Hey! Do you have this or that, could I borrow it? And you bet, you have it somewhere . . ."

Mashed Potatoes

2 med. potatoes
1 Tbsp. sour cream
2 Tbsp. butter
½ c. milk
salt to taste

Peel and cube potatoes, cook in water till tender when pricked with a fork. Drain off all water. Mash with a potato-masher or put in blender. Mash till all lumps are gone. Add sour cream and butter. Mix well. Add milk and salt; and mix again. Put pan of mashed potatoes back on stove on low heat, stirring constantly till hot. If too thick add more milk. Ready to serve with chicken and gravy.

Mashed Potatoes

1 env. Martha White spud flakes
evaporated milk, optional
3 Tbsp. sour cream
4 butter

Use milk instead of water. Heat milk according to directions on package. Add sour cream and butter last. Tastes almost like homemade.

Deep fry chicken breast and fish
at 375°. Potato wedges or thick
slices at 350°. Each piece will
float on top when done.

Meal Deluxe

2 hamburger patties, quarter pounder

2 cabbage leaves

2 tsp. chopped onions

butter

Lawry's seasoned salt

fresh vegetables (frozen or canned vegetables will do)

Take hamburger patties; sprinkle with Lawry's on both sides. Place on a tinfoil square. Place cabbage leaf on top of hamburger. This is your bowl to put the vegetables in. Put ¾ cup vegetables, onions and a dab of butter in leaf. Sprinkle with salt. Seal in foil by folding together opposite corners. Bring two last corners over first two. Press all edges together to seal. Bake at 375° for 35 minutes or until meat and vegetables are done. Put on serving plate and eat with sour cream. If using froxen patties, extend baking time.

Rice and Raisins

1½ c. milk

2 Tbsp. brown sugar or maple syrup

½ tsp. vanilla

½ c. rice

½–¾ c. raisins

Bring milk, sugar and vanilla to a boil. Add rice and bring to a boil again. Cover; turn off heat. Let set 10 minutes. Fluff with fork and bring to a boil again: let set until desired doneness, about 45 minutes. After about 30 minutes put raisins in small pan, add water to cover. Simmer until very soft. Reheat rice and raisins to steaming. Spoon rice on plate, sprinkle with brown sugar, top with raisins. Serve with pan fried liver, fried in the iron skillet. Rice and raisins were made in the heavy bottom "Lifetime Cookware." If you use lightweight cookware, you may have to simmer the rice and add more hot milk. When I was a little girl back in the 50's and 60's, this was a favorite supper meal during the winter.

Dressing

2 pieces bread, cubed and toasted
1 egg, beaten
¾ c. milk
¼ c. cubed, cooked potatoes
¼ c. cut-up, cooked carrots
¼ c. chopped celery, optional
1 tsp. Lawry's seasoned salt
½ tsp. chicken base
dash of pepper
1 tsp. salt

Mix all ingredients together. Set aside for 15 minutes. Put four tablespoons butter in skillet and melt. Add ingredients and fry to desired doneness. Dried vegetables may be used instead of fresh vegetables. Serve with mashed potatoes and gravy.

Pan Fried Chicken over Rice

2 pieces chicken breast
4 Tbsp. butter
Lawry's seasoned salt
1 c. water
½ c. rice, uncooked
2 tsp. chicken base

Melt butter in small saucepan. Roll chicken in flour and put in pan. Sprinkle top with Lawry's seasoned salt. Meanwhile bring water to a boil. Add rice and chicken base. Stir and bring to a rolling boil, put cover on. Turn off heat. Let set on stove. Do not remove lid till ready to serve. When chicken is golden brown turn once and sprinkle with Lawry's. When chicken is one-half done, add ½ cup boiling water and cover. Simmer 20–30 minutes or till chicken is done. Spoon rice on plates and put chicken breast on rice. Spoon chicken broth over top. Chicken can be cut into bite-size pieces before serving.

Fried Chicken

4 pieces chicken legs and thighs

1 egg, beaten

¼ c. milk

⅓ c. flour

½ tsp. salt

⅛ tsp. pepper

2 c. crushed saltine cracker crumbs

Take skin off chicken, dry on paper towel. Mix egg, milk, flour, salt and pepper together. Put cracker crumbs in separate dish. Dip chicken into batter then roll into cracker crumbs. Fry in skillet, using 1 cup of butter. Adding more butter if necessary. Fry till golden brown. Additional salt may be added when frying. Put in a roaster and add ½ cup water. Bake in oven at 350° for 20–30 minutes or till tender when pricked with a fork.

Good Crunchy Chicken

2 pieces boneless, skinless chicken breast

1 egg, beaten

¼ c. milk, scant

¼ c. crushed cornflakes

¼ c. crushed saltine crackers

Lawry's seasoned salt

dash of pepper

Dip chicken in egg and milk mixture, then roll into crumbs. Line casserole with foil. Put chicken on top of foil. Add ¼ cup water. Put lid on casserole, or put double layer of paper towel in bottom of casserole, line with foil, cut three slits in foil bottom. Cover roaster tightly with foil and bake chicken until done. Do 6–8 pieces of chicken. It is good reheated.

A big slotted spoon works better for deep frying than meat tongs.

Baked Chicken Breast

boneless, skinless chicken breast or boneless thighs

salt and pepper

½ c. butter

saltine cracker crumbs

Salt and pepper the chicken. Melt butter. Dip chicken in butter; roll in cracker crumbs. Bake on a cookie sheet at 350° for 35–45 minutes. Serve on a bed of rice. Top with sweet and sour sauce. Or serve with mashed potatoes and vegetables.

Baked Chicken

2 piece boneless, skinless chicken breast

salt and pepper

⅔ c. sauerkraut

2 slices Swiss cheese

½ c. Thousand Island salad dressing

Place chicken in a greased pan. Sprinkle with salt and pepper. Press excess liquid from sauerkraut. Spoon kraut over chicken. Top with cheese slices. Pour dressing evenly over top. Cover pan with lid or foil. Bake at 325° for 1½ hours or until chicken is tender.

Mexican Chicken and Rice

2 pieces boneless, skinless chicken breasts, cut in bite-sized pieces

1 tsp. chili powder

1 c. chunky salsa

½ c. water

¾ c. rice

Melt one tablespoon butter in skillet. Sprinkle chili powder over cut-up chicken and fry in skillet until tender. Add salsa and water. Bring to a boil and add rice. Mix thoroughly. Cover. Remove from heat. Let stand 15–20 minutes. Serve with applesauce.

Chicken Supreme

½ c. diced chicken, cooked

½ c. uncooked macaroni

½ c. milk

¼ c. grated cheese

pinch of salt

dash of pepper

1 tsp. butter

1 Tbsp. minced onions

½ c. cream of chicken soup

Combine, milk, cheese, seasonings, butter, onions and soup. Heat until cheese is melted. Cool. Pour over macaroni and chicken in casserole. Bake at 350° for 1½ hours or till macaroni is tender. Can be prepared evenings before and refrigerated overnight and baked the next day.

Crispy Fried Chicken

1 c. all-purpose flour, divided

1½ tsp. garlic salt

¾ tsp. paprika

¾ tsp. pepper, divided

¾ tsp. poultry seasoning or Lawry's

1 egg

⅜ c. water

¼ tsp. salt

¾–1 lb. frying chicken or chicken breast, cut up

cooking oil for deep-fat frying

In a resealable plastic bag or shallow bowl, combine ½ cup flour, garlic salt, paprika, half of the pepper and poultry seasoning. In another bowl, beat egg and water. Add salt and remaining flour. Dip chicken in egg mixture, shake or dredge in flour mixture. Fry chicken in deep fat fryer at 365° about 10 minutes.

Fried Rabbit

1 rabbit, cut up

1 c. flour

1½ c. butter

salt and pepper to taste

onion slices, optional

In a large frying pan, melt butter. Roll pieces of meat in flour and fry till brown. Put meat in a casserole. Add remaining flour to frying pan and mix well with butter till very brown. Slowly add 1–1½ quart hot water. Stir constantly with metal spatula till no lumps remain. If too thick, add more water. Season with salt and pepper to taste. This is gravy which you pour over meat in casserole. A few onion slices can be added to casserole. Bake at 325° to desired doneness. Serve with mashed potatoes and a salad. Serve rabbit gravy over mashed potatoes.

Venison Tenderloin

2 venison tenderloin

2–4 sm. onion slices, optional

1 c. butter

flour

salt and pepper to taste

Brown butter in 10" iron skillet. Meanwhile cut tenderloin into bite-size pieces; roll into flour; put in skillet and add onion slices. Fry till brown. Add 2 cups boiling water and simmer with lid on for 25 minutes or till tender, stirring occasionally. Serve over rice, mashed potatoes or a slice of homemade bread topped with butter.

Venison Burgers

1 lb. deer burger

1 sm. onion, cut up

Lawry's seasoned salt to taste

2 eggs

½ c. cracker crumbs or quick oats

Mix all together adding enough water to form into patties. Roll in flour. Fry in plenty of brown butter. Very tasty!

Easy cleanup for the barbecue grill rack: lay rack on the lawn overnight. The dew and enzymes in the grass make rack easy to clean the next morning. Works for oven racks too!

Sloppy Joe

2 c. hamburger, fried and drained

2 c. tomato cocktail

¼ c. flour

½ tsp. minced onions

1 Tbsp. barbecue sauce

2 Tbsp. brown sugar

4 tsp. chili seasoning

Fry hamburger and pour off any grease. Add tomato cocktail and flour. Stir till flour lumps are gone. Add rest of ingredients, stirring constantly till well mixed. This is also good to serve on hot dogs for coneys.

Sloppy Joe

1 lb. hamburger, fried

2 Tbsp. ketchup

1 tsp. mustard

½ c. medium salsa

2 Tbsp. brown sugar

½ tsp. Tabasco sauce

salt to taste

Fry hamburger and drain off all grease. Add all ingredients and heat over low heat, stirring constantly. Serve on a bun topped with a slice of cheese. Tomato cocktail can be used instead of salsa, or plain tomato juice. Add a little bit of this and that. Come up with your own special flavor. If joe is too sloppy, sprinkle on a little bit of flour and heat thoroughly.

Tater Tot Casserole

1 c. fried hamburger

1 c. mixed vegetables

½ c. cream of mushroom soup

¼ c. sour cream

Velveeta cheese slices

Tater Tots

Fry hamburger, drain. Put hamburger in casserole; add mixed vegetables. Spread mushroom soup and sour cream over vegetables. Top with a layer of cheese slices. Put on a layer of Tater Tots. Bake at 350° for 45 minutes to 1 hour.

Hamburgers

1 lb. hamburger

1 egg

¼ c. tomato cocktail

5 saltine crackers, crushed

1 Tbsp. barbecue sauce

½ tsp. minced onions

salt and pepper to taste

Mix ingredients together; form four patties. Put a half cup butter in skillet and melt. Coat patties with flour on both sides and put in skillet. Sprinkle with Lawry's seasoned salt. Fry on both sides till nice and brown, turning only once. Sprinkle second side with Lawry's. When done, put in small roaster or casserole. Add ½ cup water. Cover, put in oven at 200–250° to keep hot till rest of meal is ready. Gravy: To the grease you have left in skillet, add ¼ cup flour and brown till fairly dark. Add 1½ cup boiling water, stirring constantly. If too thick, add more water or juice from hamburgers when ready to serve. Salt and pepper to taste. Serve over mashed potatoes and dressing. These burgers can also be made on your grill. Brush with barbecue sauce. For a super burger sandwich; add lettuce, onion, tomato, mayo, pickles. Enjoy!

Creamed Peas over Toast

1–2 c. frozen or fresh peas
1½ c. cold milk
3 Tbsp. flour
2 tsp. sugar
¼ tsp. salt

Cook peas to desired doneness and drain off water, put back on stove over medium heat. Immediately add milk mixture, stirring constantly. Bring to almost boiling. Let set 5 minutes. If too thick, add a little hot milk. Serve over toast along with applesauce.

Poor Man's Steak

¾ lb. hamburger
¼ c. saltine cracker crumbs
¼ c. cold water
salt and pepper to taste
a dash of onion or garlic salt
½ can cream of mushroom soup
½ can water

Mix everything together except mushroom soup and water. Press in a pan to ½" thickness. Refrigerate overnight. Cut in small squares. Roll in flour and fry in butter until brown. Layer in casserole and pour the gravy mixture over meat, mushroom soup and water. Bake at 300° for 30 minutes. This can be prepared the day before and refrigerated. Have at room temperature before putting it in the oven.

Meat Loaf

1¾ lb. hamburger

1 egg

2 oz. tomato cocktail

5 saltine crackers, crushed

1 Tbsp. barbecue sauce

½ tsp. minced onions

salt and pepper to taste

Mix all ingredients. Press in small loaf pan. Bake uncovered at 350° for 45 minutes. Spread ketchup on top and bake an additional 10–15 minutes. Cut in four pieces to serve.

Meat Loaf

¾ lb. hamburger

⅓ c. oatmeal

⅓ c. tomato juice

1 egg

chopped onions, optional

1 tsp. salt

½ tsp. pepper

Topping:

1 Tbsp. ketchup

1 Tbsp. mustard

1 Tbsp. brown sugar

Mix all ingredients; press in small loaf pan. Bake 45 minutes. Meanwhile mix ingredients for topping. Pour off any grease on the meat loaf; cover with ketchup mixture and bake another 10 minutes.

Pineapple Ham Loaf

1 egg
¼ c. milk
½ c. finely crushed saltines
dash of pepper
1 lb. cooked ham, ground or ½ lb. fresh pork ground

Sauce:
½ c. brown sugar
3 Tbsp. vinegar
½ tsp. mustard
1 (4 oz.) can crushed pineapple, undrained

Mix all ingredients together and shape into a loaf. Place in a shallow baking dish. Mix ingredients for sauce and pour over loaf. Bake at 350° for 1 hour. Baste frequently during baking.

Haystacks

Ritz crackers, crushed
lettuce, shredded
rice
hard-boiled eggs, chopped
onions, chopped
fried hamburger with spaghetti sauce or sloppy joe
tomatoes, cut up
shredded cheddar cheese
Doritos, crushed

You may add or subtract ingredients. It is a very satisfying meal. Top with Golden Cheese Sauce (on next page).

Rice for Haystacks

1 c. water

1 Tbsp. butter

1 c. instant rice

Bring water and butter to a boil. Add rice. Cover and let set 10 minutes.
Fluff with a fork. Ready to serve.

Seasoned Rice for Haystacks or Stir Fry

Seasoned rice can be bought at your local grocery, Uncle Ben's Rice. Use
2 cups water to 1 cup rice. Bring water to a boil, add rice. Stir to evenly
distribute in the water. Bring back to a boil. Put lid on, turn off heat. Let set
4–5 minutes. Water should all be used up and rice should be fluffy. Make
in a heavy bottom saucepan.

Golden Cheese Sauce

½ lb. Velveeta, cut up

½ c. milk

Heat in saucepan over low heat till cheese is melted and smooth. Use on
vegetables, fish or haystacks. Yield: approximately 1 cup.

Sour cream will curdle if it becomes too hot.
Always add sour cream at the end of the
cooking time. Heat it only until it is warm—not
hot—and never to a boil.

Mac-N-Cheese

½ c. hamburger

1 c. water

⅔ c. salsa

¼ tsp. chili powder, optional

⅔ c. macaroni

Velveeta cheese

Fry hamburger, drain. Add water, salsa and chili powder. Bring to a boil; add macaroni. Stir thoroughly, cover with lid and let set 15–20 minutes or until macaroni is tender. Top with Velveeta cheese slices. For Cheeseburger Macaroni: add 2 tablespoons ketchup, 1 teaspoon onion powder, ½ teaspoon mustard. For Tomato Macaroni and Hamburger: add 2 cups tomato cocktail, 4 tablespoons brown sugar and grated Parmesan cheese for topping.

Macaroni

2 c. water

pinch of salt

1 c. macaroni

1 c. milk

Miracle Whip

Velveeta cheese

Bring water and salt to a boil. Add macaroni. Stir. Bring to a boil. Cover and let set 10 minutes. Stir and check desired doneness. Drain off water; add milk, reheat and add Miracle Whip to your taste, or add slices of Velveeta cheese and stir until melted.

Cheesy Noodles

1 ½ c. water

½ tsp. salt

½ c. crushed noodles

½ c. fried hamburger

6 slices Velveeta cheese, cut up

⅓ c. milk

Bring water to a boil, add salt and dry noodles. Cover and let set for 10–15 minutes. Drain, add hamburger, Velveeta cheese and milk. Reheat till noodles are hot and cheese is melted. Do not boil. If too thick add a little more milk.

Chicken Flavored Noodles

1 ¼ c. water

1 tsp. chicken base

1 c. noodles

Bring water to a boil, add noodles and chicken base. Bring back to boiling. Cover and let set for 15–20 minutes. Add salt to taste. When ready to serve, a slice of Velveeta cheese may be added.

Each moment of the year has its own beauty...
a picture which was never seen before and which shall never be seen again.

Roast Beef

3 lb. roast beef

2 tsp. pepper

1 Tbsp. salt

¼ c. barbecue sauce

¼ c. ketchup

1 Tbsp. steak sauce

1 Tbsp. Worcestershire sauce

4 c. tomato juice or tomato cocktail

¼ c. brown sugar

2 Tbsp. minced onions

Put in a roaster with lid for 3 hours at 250° or until meat can be pulled apart with a fork. Baste with juices several times throughout the roasting time.

Dandelion Gravy

potatoes

2 hard-boiled eggs

½ lb. bacon

¼ c. flour

1½–2 c. milk or water

salt to taste

vinegar to taste

1 c. young dandelion, cut up

Peel and cube enough potatoes for 2 people. While potatoes are cooking and eggs being hard boiled, make your gravy. Fry bacon to crisp. Drain on paper towel. Add flour to bacon drippings and fry until nice and brown. Slowly add hot milk or water, stirring briskly until no lumps remain. Season with salt and vinegar. Add dandelion greens. Serve over potato cubes and chopped egg.

Tomato Gravy

1 c. tomato cocktail

pinch of soda

¾ c. milk

3 Tbsp. flour

Bring tomato cocktail to a boil. Add soda (this keeps cocktail from becoming curdly when milk is added.) Mix milk and flour together till all lumps are dissolved. Add slowly to tomato cocktail, stirring constantly. Bring to a boil. Serve over pan fried potatoes or Saltine crackers. Sprinkle with brown or white sugar or maple syrup. Tomato cocktail recipe in Canning & Freezing section.

Old Fashioned Skillet Gravy

After you're done frying chicken or hamburgers, add 2 tablespoons flour to the 8" skillet you're using and fry until brown. Stir constantly so it won't scorch. Slowly add hot water, stirring constantly until you have your desired thickness. Season with salt and pepper etc. if needed. Simple and easy gravy, like Great Grandma used to make. "Nothing was wasted!"

Hamburger Gravy

2 potatoes

1 c. hamburger

chopped onions, optional

2 Tbsp. flour, heaping

2 c. hot milk

salt and pepper to taste

2 hard-boiled eggs

Scrub and cube potatoes; boil in salt water till tender. Meanwhile, fry hamburger and onion till well browned. Add flour and mix well. Gradually add milk to desired thickness. Add salt and pepper to taste. Eggs may be hard-boiled earlier in the day. Put cubed potatoes on plate, topped with sliced egg. Top with gravy. Serve with applesauce.

Gravy

1½ c. potato water

1 Tbsp. chicken base

½ tsp. Lawry's salt

4 Tbsp. flour

Put all together and bring to a boil, stirring constantly until thickened. If too thick add a little hot water. Note: Potato water is the water drained off from potatoes that have been cooked for mashed potatoes.

Ham Gravy

1 c. chopped ham

1 c. ham juice

2 Tbsp. clear jel

Mix all three ingredients in saucepan. Bring to a rolling boil, stirring constantly. Turn off heat. Add more salt if needed. Serve over fried potato cakes, mashed potatoes or homemade bread topped with butter.

Chicken Gravy

¾ c. chicken broth

½ c. milk, divided

1 egg yolk

1 Tbsp. clear jel

In small saucepan bring chicken broth and ¼ cup milk to a rolling boil. Take ¼ cup milk, egg yolk and 1 tablespoon clear jel and mix till no lump remains. Slowly pour milk and egg mixture into boiling broth, stirring continually till smooth.

Off the Bone Ham

Preheat oven to 250°. Put ham in foil and place in a roasting pan. An oven bag works too. Pour 20 ounces of 7-Up, Sierra Mist or Sprite over the ham and seal tightly. Bake 5 hours. The ham will stay very juicy. For a different flavor, try Pepsi.

Peach Glaze for Ham

¼ c. peach preserves

1 Tbsp. brown sugar

1 Tbsp. mustard

¼ tsp. pepper

Enough for three pounds fully cooked ham. Slice ham. Put in a roaster. Bake for 3–4 hours at 300°. Baste occasionally.

Barbecue Ham

12 slices chip chop ham

¼ c. barbecue sauce

¾ c. tomato cocktail

3 Tbsp. ketchup

2 Tbsp. Worcestershire sauce

3 Tbsp. brown sugar

Mix together in a casserole dish. Bake covered at 350° for 30 minutes. Serve on buns with a slice of Swiss cheese.

Use apple cider vinegar in your recipes. It gives a distinctive flavor.

Ground Beef Grand Style

1 lb. hamburger, fried
8 oz. cream cheese
1 can mushroom soup
1½ c. milk
½ c. ketchup
biscuits or Tater Tots

Mix all ingredients together, put in a casserole or cake pan and top with biscuits or Tater Tots. Bake at 350° until biscuits are brown or Tater Tots are golden.

A person with a healthy
attitude is too busy to worry during
the day, and too sleepy
to worry during the night!

Sour Cream Meatballs

Meatballs:

1½ c. hamburger

8 saltine crackers, crushed

1 egg

3 Tbsp. milk

⅛ tsp. ginger

salt and pepper to taste

1 Tbsp. chopped onions or ½ tsp. minced onions

¼ c. beef broth or ½ tsp. beef soup base in ¼ c. hot water

Sour Cream Sauce:

pinch of salt

pinch of ginger

1 tsp. soy sauce

2 tsp. flour

¼ c. beef broth

¼ c. sour cream

1 tsp. butter

sesame seeds, optional

Mix first seven ingredients together. Form in 1" balls. Heat butter in skillet and fry meatballs till brown. Drain fat. Add beef broth. Cover and simmer 5–10 minutes. Meanwhile prepare sauce. Mix together in saucepan: salt, ginger, soy sauce, flour and beef broth. Bring to a boil stirring constantly till thick. Remove from heat; pour into a small bowl, add sour cream and butter; stir till smooth. Place hot meatballs in serving bowl; top with sauce. Sprinkle with sesame seeds.

German Pizza

1 med. potato, shredded
½ c. fried hamburger
1 egg, beaten

Fry potatoes in a skillet till tender, don't stir. Season with pepper and Lawry's seasoned salt. Put hamburger on top of potatoes. Cook 20 minutes covered. Pour egg over meat; let egg set. Add pizza toppings, as desired: onions, peppers, mushrooms, cheese, etc. Cut like pizza.

Pizza Bubbles

1½ c. spaghetti sauce
½ can mushroom soup
½ c. pizza sauce
1½ c. hamburger or sausage, fried
1 can crescent rolls or 4 biscuits
peppers, cut up
onions, chopped
mushrooms
pepperoni
cheese

Combine spaghetti sauce, mushroom soup and pizza sauce in bowl. Add fried hamburger or sausage, peppers, onions, mushrooms and pepperoni. Stir. Cut crescent rolls in small pieces and add. Mix together and put in small casserole and bake at 400° for 20 minutes. Remove from oven and add your favorite cheese. Return to oven until cheese is melted. Serve with a salad. Delicious!

Pizza Casserole

½ lb. hamburger

1 tsp. salt

¼ tsp. garlic

⅛ tsp. pepper

½ tsp. oregano

4 oz. Inn Maid noodles

¼ lb. mozzarella cheese, grated

1 sm. can pizza sauce

Fry hamburger; drain. Cook noodles in salt water and drain. Add seasonings to hamburger. Mix noodles and pizza sauce. Put mixture in casserole dish. Sprinkle cheese on top. Bake uncovered at 350° for 30 minutes. You can also add pepperoni, mushrooms, onions and green peppers. This is a dish that has more flavor second time around.

Beef Stew

1 lb. beef chunks

1 sm. onion, chopped

1 sm. carrot, chopped

1 c. diced celery

1½ c. cubed potatoes

¼ c. butter

Roll beef chunks in flour and brown in skillet along with onions. Melt butter in skillet before adding meat and onions. When meat is browned add 4 cups hot water cover and simmer for 1 hour. Add vegetables and simmer for another hour, adding more hot water if needed. Salt and pepper to taste. Seasonings can be added when frying meat and onions. Cast iron Dutch oven works well on your stove, or the cast iron skillet.

Stew

1 pt. canned steak or chunk meat, chopped

1½ c. water

2 oz. noodles

1 potato, diced

1 carrot, diced

chopped onion, optional

1 c. canned corn

1 c. canned beans

salt to taste

Bring first two ingredients to a boil. Add noodles. Simmer 10 minutes, then add potato, carrot and onion. Simmer another 3–4 minutes. Add corn and beans. Simmer 10 more minutes. Add salt. Leftovers make another great meal. Use Dutch oven, tastes like outdoor cooking.

A friend is one who knows all *about you and still loves you!*

Vegetable Pizza

Crust:

¼ c. butter

2 Tbsp. sugar

½ c. boiling water

1 Tbsp. yeast

¼ c. warm water

1 egg, beaten

1 ½ c. flour

1 tsp. salt

Filling:

1 (8 oz.) cream cheese

1 ½ c. Miracle Whip

16 oz. sour cream

dash of onion or garlic powder

1 pkg. Hidden Valley Ranch mix

dried beef, chopped fine

broccoli

carrots

tomatoes, pea size

cauliflower

shredded cheese

bacon bits

red, yellow, green peppers

Crust: Combine first three ingredients. Stir and cool to lukewarm. Dissolve yeast in warm water. Add to butter and sugar mixture. Add egg, flour and salt. Mix well, let rise 10 minutes. Divide dough and put on two 8"x12" cookie sheets. Bake at 325° 10–15 minutes. When cold, cover one pan and put away for later. Store in a cool place. Filling: Mix well, spread half of the mixture on one crust. Put other half in a tight container and refrigerate. Add different kinds of vegetables to decorate your pizza. Note: If you are a grandma with lots of time, use a paring knife and cut the cauliflower and broccoli into small flowerets, or use salsa master.

Zucchini Fritters

1 c. grated zucchini
1 c. grated carrots
2 Tbsp. chopped onions
½ c. flour
¼ tsp. salt
¼ tsp. pepper
⅛ tsp. seasoned salt

Drop by teaspoonfuls into hot buttered skillet. Fry slowly till vegetables are tender. Serve with gravy or pancake syrup.

Chicken and Vegetable Fry

1 c. cooked and diced chicken
¾ c. diced carrots
¾ c. diced potatoes
¾ c. diced celery
2 Tbsp. butter
1 Tbsp. flour
1 Tbsp. diced green peppers, optional

In a skillet, melt butter. Add flour. Stir till flour is mixed with butter. Add chicken, well drained vegetables and peppers. Fry till crisp and brown, turning to brown evenly. Serve with applesauce or sour cream.

How strange this fear of death is.
We are never frightened at a sunset.

Vegetable Stir Fry

3 Tbsp. butter
2 Tbsp. flour
½ c. canned corn, drained
½ c. canned peas, drained
½ c. green beans, drained
½ c. canned lima beans, drained
1–2 hot dogs, chopped
salt to taste
1 tsp. chopped onions, optional
Velveeta cheese slices, optional

Melt butter in iron skillet. Add flour and brown slightly. Add all but Velveeta cheese. Fry till golden brown, stirring occasionally. Top with Velveeta cheese slices. Serve with sour cream or applesauce.

Steamed Vegetables

1 c. baby carrots, cut in half
1 c. cauliflower, cut up flowerets
3 slices Velveeta cheese, fairly thick

Steam vegetables for 30 minutes or till tender. Add slices of cheese and cover. Let set till cheese is melted. Serve with applesauce.

Green Beans with Ham

4 Tbsp. butter

1 Tbsp. flour, heaping

1 pt. canned green beans, drained

2 Tbsp. chopped onions

salt to taste

½ c. cubed ham

Velveeta cheese slices

Melt butter in skillet, add flour and brown slightly. Add beans, onions, salt and ham, stirring constantly until well mixed. Fry until slightly browned, stirring occasionally. Turn off heat and cover with Velveeta cheese. Put a cover on until cheese is melted. Serve with sour cream or applesauce. (Bacon bits may be used instead of ham.)

Fresh Green Beans

2 c. green beans, cut up

2 Tbsp. butter

sour cream and onion powder

Steam beans in a small saucepan. Don't boil. Meanwhile brown butter in small pan. When ready to serve beans, pour butter over beans and sprinkle with sour cream and onion powder. Serve with mashed potatoes and chicken.

Creamed Corn

1 c. canned corn, drained
¾ c. milk
1 Tbsp. flour
1 Tbsp. sugar
1 tsp. salt

Combine all ingredients in a saucepan. Bring to a boil, stirring constantly; cook until thickened. If using frozen corn, cook until desired doneness. Drain and add to milk mixture, cook until thickened.

Sauerkraut

1 c. sauerkraut, some juice squeezed out
2 hot dogs, sliced
1 Tbsp. sugar

Put kraut in casserole, add sliced hot dogs and sugar. Cover and bake at 350° for 25 minutes.

The difference between
a stumbling block and
a stepping stone is the
way a man uses them.

Sour Cream Noodle Casserole

2 c. Inn Maid noodles

1 c. hamburger

1 sm. onion, chopped

salt and pepper to taste

½ c. cream of mushroom soup

¼ c. sour cream

½ c. milk

1 Tbsp. butter

¼ c. Velveeta, optional

Cook noodles until about tender, drain. Fry hamburger and chopped onions until brown. Season with salt and pepper. Drain off fat. Meanwhile heat soup, sour cream, milk, butter and Velveeta cheese until melted. Do not boil. Mix all together and put in casserole. If too thick, add more milk. Bake at 350° for 30 minutes. Last, place cheese slices on top and melt.

Penny Pincher Casserole

3 med. potatoes, cubed

1 pt. peas, drained

¼ c. butter

1 can cream of mushroom soup

1 tsp. mustard

6 hot dogs, sliced

3 Tbsp. chopped onions

Mix all ingredients together. Put in casserole and bake at 350° for 30 minutes or until potatoes are tender.

Reuben Casserole

½ c. cream of mushroom soup

⅓ c. milk

2 Tbsp. chopped onions or ½ tsp. minced onions

1 tsp. mustard

½ c. sauerkraut

½ c. noodles, crushed

2 hot dogs or 1 polish sausage, cut in small pieces

½ c. shredded Swiss cheese

1 bread crust, broken in small pieces

2 tsp. butter

Combine soup, milk, onion and mustard in bowl. Blend well. Spread kraut in casserole, top with uncooked noodles. Spoon soup mixture evenly over top. Top with sausage, then cheese. Combine bead crumbs and butter in small bowl. Sprinkle on top. Put lid on and bake at 350° for 35 minutes or till noodles are tender.

Potato Casserole

2 eggs, beaten

2 med. potatoes, cubed

¼ c. milk

¼ c. chopped onions

¼ c. dry bread crumbs

salt and pepper to taste

½ c. shredded cheddar cheese

4 strips of bacon, cooked and crumbled

In a bowl, beat eggs; stir in potatoes, milk, onions, bread crumbs, salt and pepper. Put in a quart baking dish. Bake at 350° for 30 minutes or until potatoes are tender. Top with cheese and crumbled bacon. Return to oven until cheese is melted.

Sweet Potato Casserole

1 c. mashed sweet potatoes
5 tsp. butter
5 tsp. sugar
1 egg, beaten
¼ tsp. vanilla
5 tsp. milk

Topping:
1 Tbsp. butter
⅓ c. brown sugar
5 tsp. flour
nuts, optional

Mix first six ingredients and pour in casserole. Sprinkle topping over top and bake uncovered at 350° for 25 minutes or until done.

Leftover Christmas Casserole

½ c. sauerkraut
½ c. noodles
½ c. ham, chopped
½ c. mashed potatoes
¾ c. ham gravy

Layer in a casserole, put gravy on top. Heat in a 350° oven for 20 minutes or thoroughly heat. Serve with applesauce.

Leftover Mashed Potato Casserole

1 c. vegetable soup
1½ c. mashed potatoes
Swiss cheese slices or shredded cheddar cheese

Put soup in bottom of casserole, top with mashed potatoes. Last add cheese. Bake at 350° till thoroughly heated.

Leftover Meal

1 c. leftover cheesy noodles
1 c. leftover mixed vegetables
2 leftover barbecue hot dogs, sliced
¼ c. milk

Mix all together, put in a saucepan and heat. Do not boil. Spoon on your plate and top with a slice of Velveeta cheese.

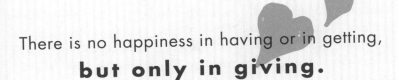

There is no happiness in having or in getting,
but only in giving.

 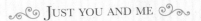

Leftover Casserole

Monday morning coffee break—hamburger salsa dip

Tuesday supper— cooked and cubed potatoes, bologna, corn, gravy

Wednesday supper—stuffed peppers with leftover hamburger salsa dip and rice

Thursday supper—fix casserole

Cube the bologna, chop the stuffed peppers put in layers in casserole, add some frozen mixed vegetables and gravy on top. Bake at 350° until heated thoroughly. Top with Velveeta cheese or shredded cheddar, put back in oven until cheese is melted. Serve with sour cream and apple sauce. I've served a casserole like this to a friend that happened to stop by. Tastes as good as new! Try it! Grandma always said: "No waste, no want!"

Leftover Pot Pie

1 double pie crust

leftovers of mashed potatoes

sausage, chopped

corn

sauerkraut

Take pastry dough same as you would for a fruit pie. Put bottom crust in pie pan. Fill pie with your leftovers. Wet edges of crust and put on top crust; seal along edge. Make sure you have some holes in top crust so steam can escape. Cut off extra pastry. Flute around the edge. Brush top with beaten egg. Bake at 350° for 45 minutes to 1 hour or until golden brown. Serve with heated leftover gravy or sour cream and applesauce. A family favorite.

Spaghetti Bake

1 c. hamburger, fried
1 c. spaghetti sauce
1 c. spaghetti, cooked and drained
1 c. mozzarella cheese
1 c. cheese, divided

Cook and drain spaghetti. Fry hamburger, season with salt. Stir in spaghetti sauce. Cook 5 minutes. Stir in spaghetti and ½ cup cheese. Put in a casserole, top with other half cup cheese and bake at 375° for 15 minutes. Let set 5 minutes before serving.

Wiener Wiches

4 hot dogs, sliced
½ c. diced or shredded cheese
½ tsp. mustard
1 tsp. ketchup
1 tsp. minced onion
1 tsp. pickle relish

Mix all ingredients together and fill hot dog buns. Wrap in foil and bake at 325° for 15–20 minutes. They may be made in advance and frozen. Allow longer baking time when frozen.

Barbecue Sauce for Chicken

½ c. vinegar

5 Tbsp. salt

1 c. butter

2 Tbsp. Worcestershire sauce

1 c. wine

Combine and keep warm enough to keep butter melted. Also good on pork chops and steaks. Very good!

Grilled Cheese Sandwich

2 slices bread

4 slices Velveeta cheese

butter

Spread butter on one side of bread slices. Place buttered side on skillet. Top with cheese slices. Last put second piece of bread on top of cheese buttered side up. Grill on skillet over medium heat till both sides are golden brown, turning once. Serve with dill pickles. Deluxe Sandwich: add a slice of ham, Swiss cheese instead of Velveeta. Top with a lettuce leaf, slice of tomato, homemade relish or barbecue peppers and onions. Yield: 1 large sandwich or cut in half for 2 smaller sandwiches.

Quick and Easy Sandwiches

1 lb. hamburger

1 Tbsp. minced onions

salt to taste

½ c. cream of mushroom soup

½ lb. Velveeta cheese

Fry hamburger; add onions, salt, soup and cheese. Stir until melted. Serve on buns. Will keep in refrigerator several days.

Easy Hot Ham and Cheese Sandwich

2 hamburger buns

4–6 slices ham

2 slices Swiss cheese

Take bottom half of bun and cover with ham and one slice cheese. Top with bun top. Wrap in foil. Put in oven at 350° for 10–15 minutes or until ham is hot and cheese is melted. Serve with a bowl of soup. Pickle slices can be added just before serving. These sandwiches can also be covered with Poppy Seed Dressing (see next recipe)

Poppy Seed Dressing

¼ c. butter

2 Tbsp. brown sugar

1 tsp. water

1 Tbsp. mustard

1 Tbsp. poppy seeds

Put ingredients in small pan and heat until melted. Put sandwiches on a 9"x9" pan. Pour dressing over sandwiches. Cover loosely with foil. Put in oven at 350° for 15–20 minutes until hot and cheese is melted. Serve while hot. So sticky, but good!

Burritos

2 (7") tortillas
½ c. hamburger, fried
¼ c. taco sauce, medium
chopped onions, optional
2 slices Velveeta cheese
chopped lettuce
salsa

Fry hamburger, drain. Add sauce and mix well. Spoon onto center of flour tortilla. Top with onions and cheese slice. Roll up and put in foil. Crimp foil edges tight. Heat in 350° oven 5 minutes or till cheese is melted. When on your plate, unfold and add 2–3 teaspoons salsa and lettuce. Refold and enjoy. These can also be eaten cold. Serve while your hamburger is hot. Spread sour cream down the center of your burrito. Add the rest of the topping. Roll up and enjoy. Optional: shredded cheddar cheese and bacon bits.

Stuffed Peppers

¾ c. fried hamburger
⅓ c. oatmeal
1 egg
2 Tbsp. chopped onions
1 tsp. salt
dash of pepper
½ c. tomato cocktail

This will stuff 3–4 medium green peppers. Pour tomato cocktail on top before baking. Bake about 1 hour.

Breading Mix

2 c. saltine cracker crumbs

2 c. Gold Medal flour (all purpose)

1 c. Bisquick

5 Tbsp. Lawry's seasoned salt

1 Tbsp. salt

2 Tbsp. sugar

2½ lb. Runion mix

Mix all together. Store in a tight container. Approximately 3 quart. When using to deep fry, first dip chicken, fish or potatoes in beaten eggs, roll in breading mix and deep fry immediately. Form your hamburger patties and roll in breading mix. Fry in a skillet. Give it a try for carrots and sweet potatoes.

Barbecue Sauce

1 sm. onion, chopped

2 Tbsp. butter

¾ c. water

½ c. ketchup

¼ c. vinegar

4 tsp. Worcestershire sauce

4 drops hot pepper sauce

4 tsp. sugar

¼ tsp. pepper

In saucepan, cook onions in butter until tender. Add remaining ingredients. Simmer uncovered for 20–30 minutes, stirring occasionally. Use when grilling hamburgers or chicken. Keep leftover sauce in refrigerator. Yield: 1 cup.

Long Time Ago

Breeze through Grandma's kitchen
Aromas did flow
Round the old cookstove
Long time ago.

Grandpa in the field a-plowing
Horses in tow
Grandchildren stood watching him
Long time ago.

Then from the front porch
Grandma called low
Dinner is on the table
Long time ago.

For in a happy home
Cooking we know
Has brought love to the kitchen
Long time ago.
-Wilma

Desserts

Glorified Rice

1 c. cooked rice

½ c. crushed pineapple

¼ c. sugar

12 miniature marshmallows

½ c. chopped apples

½ c. whipped cream

Cook rice until tender, but not mushy; cool. Mix all ingredients together except cream, and let set 1 hour. Fold whipped cream into mixture just before serving. Garnish with candied cherries. Leftover rice may be used.

Oatmeal Pone

1½ c. brown sugar

1 c. quick oatmeal

1½ c. flour

1 c. sour cream

2 eggs

1 tsp. salt

1 tsp. baking soda

Mix all ingredients together. Bake in a 9"x9" pan at 375° for 30 minutes. Serve with fresh or canned fruit and milk. Take a thick slice while warm and top with butter. Sour cream substitute: Put 2 tablespoons vinegar in cup and fill with milk.

Cream Puffs

¼ c. water

2 Tbsp. butter

¼ c. flour

1 egg

Filling Options 1:

1 envelope Dream Whip

3.4 oz. vanilla instant pudding

2 c. cold milk

1 tsp. vanilla

Filling Option 2:

3.4 oz. vanilla instant pudding

1½ c. cold milk

½ tsp. vanilla

Bring water and butter to a rolling boil. Stir in flour. Stir vigorously over low heat until mixture forms a ball. Remove from heat. Beat in egg and continue stirring until mixture is smooth. Drop dough onto ungreased cookie sheet into 4 piles. Bake at 400° until puffed and golden, about 30 minutes. Cool. Cut off tops, spoon out any soft dough. Fill puff with filling and replace tops. Sprinkle with powdered sugar. Filling: Mix together until thick. Refrigerate until ready to serve. Serve the extra pudding on the side. Yum!

The future belongs to those who believe in the beauty *of their dreams*.

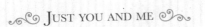

Cream Cheese Braid

Dough:
1 Tbsp. yeast
½ c. warm water
¼ c. butter, softened
2½ Tbsp. sugar
1 egg
pinch of salt
2–2¼ c. flour

Pineapple Filling:
½ c. crushed pineapple
¼ c. sugar
1½ Tbsp. clear jel

Cream Cheese Filling:
1 (8 oz.) cream cheese, softened
1 Tbsp. sugar
2 tsp. lemon juice
½ tsp. vanilla

Icing:
½ c. powdered sugar
1–2 Tbsp. milk

In a mixing bowl dissolve yeast in water, let stand for 5 minutes. Add butter, sugar, egg, salt and 1 cup flour. Mix well. Add enough remaining flour to form a soft dough. Knead on a floured surface until smooth (about 6–8 minutes). Place in a greased bowl, turning once to grease top. Cover and let rise until double, about 45 minutes. Meanwhile, combine pineapple filling ingredients in saucepan. Bring to a boil; reduce heat, cook and stir until thickened. Cool. Mix cream cheese filling and set aside. On a floured surface roll dough into a 9"x13" rectangle, place on a greased cookie sheet. Spread cream cheese filling lengthwise down center third of triangle. Spread pineapple filling on top. On each long side, cut 1" wide strips 3" into center. Starting at one end, fold alternating strips at an angle across filling. Seal ends, cover and let rise for 20 minutes. Bake at 350° for 25–30 minutes or until golden brown. Cool. If desired, drizzle icing over braid. Yield: 1 braid. Note: other pie fillings may be used in place of the pineapple filling. Our favorite is sour cherry.

Pineapple Rice Pudding

1 c. cooked rice

1 c. crushed pineapple, drained

½ c. Cool Whip

2 Tbsp. powdered sugar

¼ tsp. vanilla

1 c. fruit cocktail (optional)

In a bowl, combine rice and pineapple; set aside. In another bowl mix Cool Whip, powdered sugar and vanilla. Fold into rice mixture. Cover and chill until ready to serve. Decorate with a dab of Cool Whip, a mint sprig and/or a maraschino cherry.

A person pardons in the same degree that HE LOVES.

Pumpkin Torte

Crust:

12 crushed graham crackers

¼ c. sugar

¼ c. butter

Layer 1:

1 egg, beaten

⅓ c. sugar

4 oz. cream cheese

Layer 2:

½ Tbsp. gelatin dissolved in 2 Tbsp. cold water

1 c. pumpkin

2 eggs, separated

¼ c. sugar

¼ c. milk

¼ tsp. salt

½ Tbsp. cinnamon

2 Tbsp. sugar

4 oz. Cool Whip

Mix and press crust ingredients in 9"x9" pan. Mix layer 1 ingredients and pour over crust. Bake 20 minutes at 350°. Cool. For layer 2, cook pumpkin, egg yolks, ¼ c. sugar, milk, salt, and cinnamon together, stirring constantly until thickened. Remove from heat, add dissolved gelatin. Cool. Beat egg whites until soft peaks form, beat in 2 tablespoons sugar. Fold into pumpkin mixture. Fold in ½ of the Cool Whip. Pour over cooled crust. Spread rest of Cool Whip over top. Refrigerate 1 hour before serving.

Peach Cobbler

1 c. canned peaches

3 Tbsp. sugar, divided

1 tsp. clear jel, scant

¼ tsp. vanilla

1 Tbsp. brown sugar, heaping

¾ c. flour, divided

3 Tbsp. uncooked old fashioned rolled oats

1 Tbsp. butter

¼ tsp. cinnamon

pinch of salt

3 Tbsp. shortening

2 Tbsp. cold water

Drain peach slices, reserving 2 ounces syrup. Combine 2 tablespoons sugar and clear jel in a small saucepan. Slowly add reserved syrup, stirring to make a smooth sauce, add vanilla. Cook over low heat till thick, stirring constantly. Set aside. Combine brown sugar, ¼ cup flour, oats, butter and cinnamon in small bowl, stir until crumbly. Set aside. Combine remaining flour, sugar and salt in small bowl. Cut in butter until mixture resembles course crumbs. Sprinkle water, 1 tablespoon at time, over flour mixture and toss lightly until mixture holds together. Press together to form ball. Press into an 8"x8" pan, also up the sides. Layer peaches, sauce and crumb topping over crust. Bake at 325° for 45 minutes. Serve warm with vanilla ice cream. Delicious!

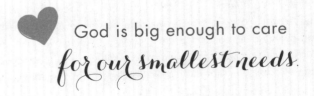

God is big enough to care
for our smallest needs.

Cobbler

1 c. flour

1 Tbsp. sugar

1½ tsp. baking powder

½ tsp. baking soda

3 Tbsp. shortening

½ c. milk

Mix dry ingredients. Cut in shortening and stir in milk. Mix well. Drop by spoonfuls onto fruit. Bake until golden brown at 400° for 25–30 minutes. Serve warm with milk. Cook your own fruit filling or use with any fruit filling in canning section.

Apple Cranberry Cobbler

½ c. evaporated milk

¾ c. flour

1½ Tbsp. butter, melted

1 tsp. baking powder

½ tsp. cinnamon

¼ tsp. salt

⅓ c. sugar

1 c. apple pie filling

½ c. dried cranberries

⅓ c. hot water

whipped topping (optional)

Combine first 7 ingredients in a bowl until just blended. Spread in a 9"x9" greased baking dish. Combine apple pie filling and cranberries and spread evenly over batter. Carefully pour hot water over fruit. Bake at 350° for 25–30 minutes. Serve warm with milk or whipped topping. Cobbler can also be served as main dish. Serve with hot dog sandwiches.

Apple Dumplings

Dough:

1 c. flour

1 ¼ tsp. baking powder

¼ tsp. salt

⅓ c. shortening

¼ c. milk

Sauce:

1 c. brown sugar

1 c. water

2 Tbsp. butter

¼ tsp. cinnamon

3 apples, peeled and cut in half

Roll out dough, cut in squares. Place 1 apple half on each square. Wet edges of dough and seal around the apple. Set the dumpling in a pan. Pour sauce over dumplings and bake at 425° until golden brown and apples are tender. Serve with milk or ice cream. My version: shred the apples, roll out dough as you would to make cinnamon rolls. Spread the shredded apples on dough and roll up starting at long side. Slice ½"–¾" thick. Put in your pan and pour sauce over top and bake. Very good!

LISTENING, NOT IMITATIONS,

may be the sincerest form of flattery.

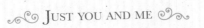

Apple Crisp

1 pt. pie filling

½ c. oatmeal

½ c. flour

⅛ tsp. baking soda

½ c. brown sugar

¼ c. butter

⅛ tsp. baking powder

Pour 1 pint pie filling in 8"x8" pan. Cover with crumbs made from remaining ingredients. Bake at 375˚ until golden brown. Serve with milk or a dish of homemade ice cream. Apple pie filling recipe is in Canning and Freezing section.

Apple Crisp

2 med. cooking apples, pared and sliced (about 2 c.)

2 Tbsp. water

3 Tbsp. flour

2 Tbsp. sugar

2 Tbsp. butter, softened

¼ tsp. cinnamon

Put apples in 8" pie pan; sprinkle water over apples. Mix flour, sugar, butter and cinnamon with a fork until crumbly. Sprinkle over apples. Bake uncovered at 350° for 25–30 minutes or till topping is golden brown and apples are tender. Serve hot with milk or ice cream.

Grandma's Baked Caramel Apples

1 Tbsp. butter

1 Tbsp. flour

1 c. brown sugar

1 c. boiling water

pinch of salt

½ tsp. vanilla

Melt butter in iron skillet, add flour and brown, stirring constantly with a flat spatula. Add brown sugar slowly. Add boiling water, salt and vanilla. Stir until smooth and thickened. Peel, pare and halve 2 or 3 large apples. Fit them in a baking pan, side by side. Pour sauce over apples. Bake at 400° for 30–35 minutes or until apples are soft, but not mushy. Serve warm or cold. Top with whipped cream.

Baked Apples

1 Yellow Delicious apple per person

1 Tbsp. raisins

2 tsp. honey or maple syrup

½ tsp. cinnamon

Carefully remove core from apple, leaving the apple whole. Fill hole with raisins and honey. Sprinkle with cinnamon. Bake at 350° till apple is tender. Serve hot with vanilla ice cream or frozen yogurt.

Use sour cream, cottage cheese
and Cool Whip containers as
freezer boxes.

Rhubarb Dessert

½ c. flour

3 Tbsp. powdered sugar

¼ c. margarine, melted

2 eggs, beaten

3 Tbsp. flour

1½ c. chopped rhubarb

¾ c. sugar

¼ tsp. salt

Mix flour, powdered sugar, and margarine together, then press in a 9"x9" pan. Bake at 350° for 15 minutes. Mix together remaining ingredients and pour over baked crust. Bake at 350° for another 35 minutes.

Grandma's Old Fashioned Cracker Pudding

Crust:

10 graham crackers, crushed fine

6 Tbsp. butter, melted

½ c. sugar

Filling:

4 c. milk

½ c. sugar

½ tsp. vanilla

1 (3.4 oz.) box vanilla instant pudding

pinch of salt

2 egg yolks, beaten

¼ c. clear jel

Mix crust ingredients; press in bottom of pan. In a saucepan mix filling ingredients together; bring to a boil and cook until thickened, stirring constantly. Cool slightly, and pour over cracker crust. Refrigerate. When ready to serve, top with Cool Whip or whipped topping.

Graham Cracker Pudding

2 c. milk
⅓ c. brown or white sugar
1 tsp. vanilla
3 Tbsp. clear jel

Cook until thickened, stirring constantly. Cool. Cool Whip may be added. Layer in a glass dish, beginning with pudding, crushed graham crackers, sliced bananas. Repeat layers until all pudding is used. Refrigerate. Best when served cold.

Cream Cheese Pie Filling Dessert

6 graham crackers
2 Tbsp. sugar
1 Tbsp. butter, melted or browned
4 oz. cream cheese
2 Tbsp. powdered sugar
4 oz. Cool Whip
16 oz. pie filling, your choice

Mix crushed crackers, sugar and butter. Press in bottom of a 6"x6" pan. Mix cream cheese and powdered sugar, add Cool Whip. Spread on top of cracker crust. Top with your choice of canned pie filling.

When a person tells you,
"I'll think it over and let you know,"
you already know.

Upside Down Date Pudding

1 c. boiling water

1 c. chopped dates

1 tsp. butter

½ c. sugar

½ c. brown sugar

1 egg

1 tsp. baking soda

½ tsp. baking powder

½ tsp. salt

1½ c. flour

1 c. chopped walnuts

Brown sugar sauce:

1½ c. brown sugar

1½ c. boiling water

1 Tbsp. butter

Pour boiling water over dates and butter. Let set 10 minutes. Add sugars and egg. Mix well. Add dry ingredients, mix again. Pour into sheet pan. Slowly pour brown sugar sauce over top. Bake at 350° for 40–45 minutes. When ready to serve, cut in squares or heart cookie cutters. Flip upside down on serving platter. Top with Cool Whip.

We need some clouds in our life to make a beautiful sunset.

Date Pudding

1 c. boiling water

1 tsp. baking soda

1 c. cut-up dates

1 egg

1 Tbsp. butter

1 c. brown sugar

1 tsp. baking powder

1 c. flour

nuts (optional)

Pour water over baking soda and dates, let cool. Add egg, butter, brown sugar, baking powder and flour. Bake at 325° for 25 minutes or until done. Cool. Cut in cubes. Layer alternately in a glass bowl—pudding, whipped cream, bananas and nuts. You can freeze leftover date cake for later use.

Caramel Sauce for Date Pudding

1 c. Karo

1 c. sugar

1 c. cream, divided

1 Tbsp. butter

Mix Karo, sugar and ½ of cream together. Boil to soft ball (240°). Add rest of the cream and boil until creamy. If too stiff when cold, add hot water until desired thickness. Use approximately 1 cup sauce for a medium size bowl of date pudding. Layer cut up date cake, sliced bananas, caramel sauce, Cool Whip, and chopped nuts. Repeat layers. Any leftovers can be kept in refrigerator up to 3 weeks.

Sauce for Date Pudding

½ c. sweetened condensed milk

1 c. Cool Whip

nuts (optional)

bananas (optional)

Mix condensed milk and Cool Whip until smooth. Put a layer of date pudding in bowl, layer of banana, nuts, sauce. Repeat to fill bowl. Garnish with banana slices and nuts.

Caramel Sauce for Date Pudding

4 Tbsp. butter

2 Tbsp. flour

1 c. brown sugar

1 c. water

¼ tsp. salt

½ tsp. vanilla

Melt butter, add flour and sugar and let caramelize to light brown, stirring with spatula so it doesn't scorch. Add water, salt and vanilla. Cook until thick.

Always use cooked or canned pineapple in Jell-O salads. Fresh pineapple and kiwi will prevent Jell-O from setting.

Butterscotch Tapioca

2 c. water

pinch of salt

½ c. pearl tapioca

⅔ c. brown sugar

1 egg, beaten

3 Tbsp. sugar

⅓ c. milk

¼ tsp. vanilla

2 Tbsp. butter

Bring water and salt to a boil and add tapioca. Cook 10 minutes, add brown sugar. Mix egg, sugar, milk and vanilla together, add to tapioca mixture. Cook until it bubbles. Brown butter, add to tapioca. Cool. Add whipped cream or Cool Whip, bananas and diced Milky Way bars to your desire.

Tapioca

1½ c. water

⅓ c. sugar

⅓ c. pearl tapioca, heaping

1 c. frozen strawberries

1 tsp. strawberry Jell-O, heaping

Bring sugar and water to a rolling boil, add tapioca and stir. Bring to a boil, turn off heat; cover and let set 30 minutes. Add strawberry Jell-O. Stir until Jell-O is dissolved. Pour tapioca in a mixing bowl, add strawberries and cool. Stir occasionally. If tapioca becomes too thick, add Cool Whip to your desire. You can also make with peach Jell-O, then add crushed pineapple and peaches.

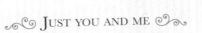

Chocolate Eclair Dessert

4 cinnamon graham crackers

1 (3 oz.) pkg. instant vanilla pudding mix

1½ c. milk

½ c. frozen whipped topping

1 square (1 oz.) semisweet chocolate

1 Tbsp. butter

½ tsp. corn syrup

1 Tbsp. milk

½ tsp. vanilla

¾ c. powdered sugar

Put 2 crackers in a 7"x7" pan to cover bottom of pan. Set aside. Combine pudding mix and milk; fold in whipped topping. Spread on crackers. Top with 2 more crackers. In a saucepan, melt chocolate and butter, remove from heat and add remaining ingredients. Spread over top of cracker layer. Cover and refrigerate. Best flavor if made 2 days ahead.

Raspberry Delight

⅓ c. raspberry Jell-O

2 c. boiling water

4 oz. cream cheese

1 Tbsp. powdered sugar, heaping

¾ c. Cool Whip

1 c. fresh raspberries, smashed slightly

chopped nuts (optional)

In a non-plastic bowl, mix Jell-O with boiling water. Stir until dissolved. Let set until Jell-O is firm. Whip Jell-O with beater. Cream together cream cheese with powdered sugar; add Cool Whip and mix with jello. Fold in raspberries and nuts. Pour in a glass bowl and refrigerate until ready to serve. Garnish with additional whole raspberries and nuts if desired. Peach Jell-O and chopped canned peaches may be substituted. A must-have come raspberry season!

Ribbon Salad

1 oz. Jell-O, 3 different flavors

¾ c. boiling water

4 oz. cream cheese

2 Tbsp. powdered sugar

½ c. Cool Whip

Take 1 ounce raspberry Jell-O, put in a non-plastic bowl and add ¾ cup boiling water. Stir till dissolved. Cool. Pour in a pan or small clear glass dish. Let set till firm. Meanwhile take orange Jell-O and repeat process. When slightly set, cream powdered sugar with cream cheese and blend in Cool Whip. Stir till smooth. Mix well with orange Jell-O. Pour onto 1st layer of set Jell-O. Let set till firm. Repeat 1st step with lime Jell-O. Jell-O needs to be cold, but still able to pour. Pour onto second layer and let set completely. Use your choice of flavors and color. Use lighter color in middle layer.

Sour Cream Jell-O Dessert

2 oz. Jell-O, your choice of flavor

10 oz. boiling water

1 Tbsp. sour cream, heaping

¾ c. banana or fruit cocktail

¼ c. chopped nuts (optional)

Pour boiling water over Jell-O. Stir till dissolved. Cool till slightly set, add sour cream, stir till mixed. Quarter bananas and slice in ¼" slices; add to Jell-O. Add nuts to Jell-O. Pour in glass dessert dishes. Refrigerate till ready to serve. Add a dab of topping. Top with a slice of banana and sprinkle with nuts. Serve. Note: Drain fruit cocktail before adding to Jell-O.

The course of nature is the art of God.

Instant Dessert

1 (3.4 oz.) box vanilla instant pudding

1½ c. cold milk

1 banana, sliced

3 graham crackers, finely crushed

1 Tbsp. sour cream, heaping (optional)

Beat pudding and milk until slightly thickened. Set aside. Meanwhile crush crackers. Just before serving add sour cream to pudding; mix well. Layer in dessert dishes beginning with pudding, crackers and banana slices. Repeat. Garnish top with banana slices.

Rainbow Jell-O Salad

16 oz. sour cream

3 oz. cherry Jell-O

3 oz. lime Jell-O

3 oz. peach Jell-O

3 oz. lemon Jell-O

3 oz. strawberry Jell-O

boiling water

cold water

Mix 1 cup boiling water with each pkg. Jell-O. Take ½ of each Jell-O and add ⅓ cup sour cream. Add ¼ cup cold water to remaining ½ cup of Jell-O. Each color makes 2 layers. 1st layer has sour cream, next is plain. Depends on size Jell-O mold. Start with cherry and end with strawberry. I use the 5 cup Bundt pan. Make sure each layer is set before adding the next layer. To remove, dip Bundt pan in hot water for 2–3 seconds. Wipe pan dry on outside. Don't let the hot water over the edge of your pan. Put a plate on top of the mold. Hold edges tight to plate and invert. Jell-O should slide right on to the plate. Serve with cottage cheese and/ or fruit. This can be done in a glass bowl. Cut in squares, and arrange on a plate to serve.

Valentine Cutouts

2 (6 oz.) pkg. cherry or raspberry Jell-O

2½ c. boiling water

1 c. cold milk

1 (3.4 oz.) box instant vanilla pudding

1 can crushed pineapple, drained (optional)

Dissolve Jell-O in boiling water, set aside for 20 minutes. In a small bowl whisk milk and pudding. Mix until smooth; about 1 minute. Quickly pour into Jell-O, whisk until blended. Pour into 9"x13" pan. Chill until set. Cut into cubes or use heart–shaped cookie cutter. Use different colors Jell-O for different occasions. Green for St. Patrick's, yellow, orange and green for Easter and spring. Orange for Thanksgiving, etc. Arrange cut-outs on a plate to serve.

I buy all flavors Jell-O in bulk at
a local bulk food store. ⅓ cup
Jell-O is same as a small box Jell-O
bought at your grocery store.

JUST YOU AND ME

Cakes, Cookies Bars & Frostings

Angel Food Cake

1 c. egg whites
1½ Tbsp. water
¾ tsp. cream of tartar
1 c. sugar
vanilla
1 c. flour

Beat egg whites, water, cream of tartar until stiff peaks form. Gradually add sugar and vanilla. Mix well. Fold in flour with a spoon. Bake in a 7" tube pan at 350° for 35–40 minutes. Other flavors can be used. Also chopped nuts, chocolate chips, or 1 tablespoon dry Jell-O.

Sponge Cake

⅓ c. all-purpose flour
2 Tbsp. clear jel
4 eggs, separated
1 tsp. water
½ tsp. vanilla
½ c. sugar, divided
¼ tsp. salt
pinch cream of tartar

Mix flour and clear jel together. Beat egg yolks until light and thick. Add water and vanilla and half of the sugar. Fold flour mixture into yolks about ⅓ at a time. Beat egg whites, salt and cream of tartar, until soft peaks form. Gradually add the last sugar. Beat until stiff peaks form. Pour yolk mixture over whites and fold together until no streaks remain. Pour into 7" tube pan. Bake at 325° for 60 minutes.

Chocolate Chiffon Cake

½ c. milk chocolate chips

½ c. hot water

5 eggs, separated

⅔ c. sugar

1 c. all-purpose flour

1 tsp. baking powder

½ tsp. salt

1 tsp. vanilla

powdered sugar

Melt chocolate in hot water; set aside. Beat egg whites in separate bowl until soft peaks form. Gradually add sugar and beat until stiff and glossy, set aside. Combine melted chocolate mixture, egg yolks, flour, baking powder, salt and vanilla in small bowl. Carefully fold chocolate mixture into egg whites until blended. Pour into a 7" tube pan. Bake at 350° for 45–50 minutes or until top springs back when lightly touched. Invert pan; cool completely. Remove from pan, sprinkle with powdered sugar.

Sour Cream Pound Cake

⅓ c. butter, softened

1 c. sugar

¾ tsp. grated orange peel

⅓ tsp. vanilla

2 eggs

⅓ c. sour cream

pinch of salt

pinch of baking soda

1 c. flour

Citrus Topping:

⅓ c. slivered orange peel

2 tsp. salt

⅓ c. orange juice

½ c. sugar, divided

⅓ c. lemon juice

1 tsp. vanilla

Cream butter and sugar. Add orange peel, vanilla and eggs. Beat until smooth. Add sour cream, salt, baking soda and flour. Pour in 7" tube pan and bake at 325° for 45 minutes. Topping: combine orange peel and salt in saucepan. Add enough water to cover; boil 2 minutes. Drain. Add orange juice and ¼ cup sugar, simmer 10 minutes. Add remaining ¼ cup sugar, lemon juice and vanilla; stir until smooth. When cake is cold invert on plate and pour topping on. Let set so it can soak in. Delicious!

I use all-purpose Gold Medal flour
unless otherwise stated.

Oatmeal Chocolate Chip Cake

¾ c. boiling water

½ c. quick oats

½ c. brown sugar

½ c. sugar

¼ c. butter

1 egg

¾ c. flour, heaping

½ tsp. baking soda

¼ tsp. salt

2 tsp. cocoa

¾ c. mini chocolate chips, divided

½ c. chopped nuts

Pour boiling water over oatmeal. Let set 10 minutes. Cream butter and sugars; add egg. Mix well. Add dry ingredients; mix well. Add half of the chocolate chips. Pour into a 9"x9" pan. Sprinkle nuts and remaining chips on top. Bake at 350° for 35 minutes or until done.

Delicious Oatmeal Cake

¾ c. boiling water

½ c. quick oats

¼ c. butter

½ c. brown sugar

½ c. sugar

1 egg

¾ c. flour

½ tsp. nutmeg

½ tsp cinnamon

½ tsp. baking soda

¼ tsp. salt

½ tsp. vanilla

Pour boiling water over oatmeal and let set 10 minutes. Cream butter and sugars well; add egg. Blend in oatmeal mixture. Fold in dry ingredients. Pour into 9"x9" pan. Bake at 350° for 35 minutes or until done. Meanwhile mix topping to be put on cake while hot. Put under broiler about 2 minutes or until brown. Yum! Ice cream must be served.

Topping #1:

⅓ c. brown sugar

3 Tbsp. butter, melted

½ c. chopped nuts

2 Tbsp. sweet cream

½ c. coconut

½ tsp. vanilla

Topping #2:

2 Tsp. Karo

½ c. brown sugar

2 Tbsp. butter

¼ c. cream

¼ c. coconut

¼ c. chopped nuts

Bring Karo, sugar, butter and cream to a boil. Then add coconut and chopped nuts. Boil 3 minutes. Pour on cake while hot and brown in broiler.

Topping #3:

½ c. sugar

¼ c. butter

½ c. milk

2 egg yolks

¾ c. coconut

½ c. chopped nuts

½ c. powdered sugar

Cook sugar, butter, milk and egg yolks until thickened. Cool. Add coconut, nuts and powdered sugar. No need to brown in broiler.

Forget the faults of others by *remembering your own.*

Rhubarb Coffee Cake

¾ c. brown sugar

¼ c. butter

1 egg

¼ tsp. baking soda

¼ tsp. salt

1 c. flour

½ c. buttermilk

½ tsp. vanilla

¾ c. rhubarb, cut up

Topping:

½ c. white sugar mixed with ½ tsp. cinnamon

Cream sugar and butter. Add egg, mix well. Add dry ingredients along with buttermilk and vanilla. Stir in rhubarb. Pour in 9"x9" square pan. Sprinkle sugar and cinnamon on top. Bake at 350° for 25–30 minutes or until done. For a more tart coffee cake, use less sugar on top. Good when served hot with milk and a sandwich.

Test doneness in cakes and bars
by sticking a toothpick in the center
and it comes out clean.

Dutch Apple Cake

⅓ c. vegetable oil

1 egg

⅔ c. sugar

¼ tsp. vanilla

⅔ c. flour

pinch of salt

¼ tsp. baking soda

½ tsp. cinnamon

1⅓ c. chopped apples

⅓ c. chopped nuts

Topping:

¼ c. sugar

¼ c. brown sugar

1 Tbsp. flour

2 Tbsp. butter

½ c. cold water

½ tsp. vanilla

Beat together first four ingredients. Add next 4 ingredients. Mix well. Fold in chopped apples and nuts. Bake in a 8" round pan at 350° for 40–45 minutes. While cake is baking, make topping. Combine ingredients in saucepan. Mix well and cook until clear and thick. As soon as cake is done, punch holes in cake with fork and pour warm sauce on hot cake.

Cakes, Cookies,
Bars & Frostings

Apple Cake

½ c. butter

1 c. sugar

1 c. applesauce

1 tsp. baking soda

1 tsp. cinnamon

½ tsp. cloves

½ tsp. salt

1 Tbsp. boiling water

1¾ c. flour

½-1 c. raisins

½ c. chopped nuts, optional

Cream together butter, sugar and applesauce. In a cup dissolve baking soda, cinnamon, salt and cloves in boiling water. Stir into butter mixture. Add flour and mix. Stir in raisins and nuts. Pour into a greased 9"x9" pan. Bake at 350° for 45 minutes. Spoon applesauce on top of each piece just before serving.

Banana Cake

⅔ c. sugar

2 Tbsp. butter

1 egg, separated

⅓ tsp. baking soda

1 tsp. baking powder

⅓ c. sweet milk

1 banana, mashed

1 egg white, beaten stiff

vanilla

Mix sugar and butter. Add beaten egg yolk. Alternate dry ingredients with milk. Add banana and beaten egg white last, and a drop of vanilla. Bake at 350° for 35 minutes.

Gingerbread Cake

½ c. honey

½ tsp. ginger

½ tsp. cinnamon

¼ tsp. cloves

1 ¼ c. flour

¼ tsp. salt

½ tsp. baking powder

½ tsp. baking soda

¼ c. brown sugar

1 egg

¼ c. vegetable oil

2 tsp. lemon juice

⅔ c. milk

Frosting:

½ c. butter

½ c. sugar

2 Tbsp. flour

½ c. milk

½ tsp. vanilla

orange peel, optional

Combine honey, ginger, cinnamon and cloves, set aside. In another bowl cream egg, sugar and oil. Add honey mixture to egg mixture, beating until almost fluffy. Add lemon juice to milk. Add flour, salt, baking soda and baking powder alternately with milk to the sugar mixture. Bake at 350° in an 8" Bundt pan for 35–40 minutes. Cool. Remove from pan. Slice in half and frost when cold. Frosting: Cream butter and sugar until light and fluffy. Set aside. In a saucepan mix flour and milk and cook over low heat until thick, stirring constantly. Cool thoroughly. Add to creamed mixture and beat until light and fluffy. Put frosting on bottom layer of cake, top with second layer of cake. Frost entire cake and garnish with grated orange peel.

Fruit Coffee Cake

½ c. butter

¾ c. sugar

2 eggs

¼ tsp. salt

½ tsp. vanilla

¾ tsp. baking powder

1½ c. flour

2 c. fruit pie filling

Frosting:

½ c. powdered sugar

2 tsp. butter

1 Tbsp. milk

Cream butter and sugar, add eggs. Beat well. Add salt, vanilla and baking powder. Mix well. Add flour. Spread ⅔ of batter in a 9"x13" pan. Cover with filling, spoon the rest of batter on top. Bake at 350° for 30–40 minutes. Glaze with powdered sugar frosting while still warm.

If edges seem hard and crusty try using nonstick pans instead of glass.

Cinnamon Pecan Coffee Cake

¼ c. butter

½ c. sugar

1 egg

½ tsp. vanilla

½ c. sour cream

¾ c. flour

½ tsp. baking soda

Sugar Mixture:

¼ c. sugar

1 tsp. cinnamon

¼ c. chopped nuts

Cream together butter and sugar. Beat in egg and mix well. Add vanilla, sour cream, flour and soda. Pour half of batter in greased and floured 8" pan. Top with half of sugar mixture. Spoon on remaining batter and sprinkle with rest of sugar mixture. Bake at 350° for 20 minutes or until done.

Always have butter at
room temperature.

Finnish Coffee Cake

⅔ c. sugar

½ c. vegetable oil

1 egg

½ tsp. vanilla

½ c. buttermilk

1 c. flour

¼ tsp. salt

¼ tsp. baking powder

¼ tsp. baking soda

2 Tbsp. brown sugar

2 tsp. cinnamon

Glaze:

1 c. powdered sugar

2 tsp. vanilla

hot water to make drizzling consistency

Beat together sugar, oil, egg, vanilla and buttermilk. Add flour, salt, baking powder and soda. Mix well. Pour half of batter into greased 8"x8" pan. Combine sugar and cinnamon; sprinkle half on batter. Pour rest of batter on top and sprinkle with remaining sugar-cinnamon mixture. Bake at 350° for 30–35 minutes. When done, poke holes in cake with a fork and drizzle with glaze while hot.

1-2-3 Coffee Cake

1⅓ c. brown sugar

½ c. vegetable oil

½ tsp. baking soda

½ tsp. salt

½ tsp. vanilla

1 egg

½ c. warm coffee

1½ c. flour

Mix in order given. Mix well. Add flour, and mix well. Pour into a 9"x13" cookie sheet. Sprinkle with chocolate chips and chopped nuts. Bake at 350° for 25–30 minutes.

Hickory Nut Cake

¼ c. butter

¾ c. sugar

½ c. milk

½ tsp. vanilla

1½ tsp. baking powder

pinch of salt

1 c. flour

2 egg whites

⅓ c. chopped nuts

Cream butter and sugar. Add milk and vanilla. Mix well. Add baking powder, salt and flour. Fold in 2 egg whites (beaten into stiff peaks). Add nuts. Bake at 350°.

Pineapple Cake

1 egg
1 c. flour
1 c. sugar
½ tsp. vanilla
pinch of salt
1 tsp. baking soda
1 c. crushed pineapple, undrained
½ c. nuts

Icing:
4 oz. cream cheese
¼ c. butter or margarine
½ tsp. vanilla
¾ c. powdered sugar

Mix all cake ingredients together. Add 1 cup undrained, crushed pineapple. Add ½ cup nuts. Bake at 350° for 35–40 minutes in a 9"x9" pan. Cream the cream cheese and butter together. Add vanilla, last add powdered sugar. Cream together and spread on warm cake.

Pineapple Poke Cake

1 yellow Jiffy cake mix
1 (10 oz.) can crushed pineapple, drained

Topping 1:
4 oz. cream cheese, softened
⅓ c. instant vanilla pudding
½ c. cold milk

Topping 2:
1 c. whipped topping
coconut or chopped nuts

Bake cake according to package directions. Bake in a 9"x9" pan. Cool cake thoroughly. Punch large holes over top of cake with handle of a wooden spoon. Pour drained pineapple over and spread to cover and fill holes. Spread whipped topping on next. Sprinkle coconut and nuts over whipped topping. Refrigerate ½ hour. Cut in squares and serve.

Simple Chocolate Cake

(Lazy Grandma's Cake)
¾ c. flour
1½ Tbsp. cocoa
pinch of salt
½ tsp. baking soda
½ c. sugar
¼ c. vegetable oil
½ tsp. vanilla
½ c. water

Mix first 5 ingredients in bowl. Make a hole in the center and add last 3 ingredients. Mix thoroughly. Pour in a 9"x9" pan. Bake at 350° for 25–30 minutes or until done.

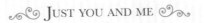

Cheesecake

Crust:

¾ c. graham cracker crumbs

2½ Tbsp. butter, softened

Filling:

4 oz. cream cheese, softened

3 oz. instant lemon pudding

1 c. milk

Mix cracker crumbs and butter. Press in bottom and sides of 8" pie pan. Mix cream cheese, pudding mix and milk. Pour in crust. Chill before serving.

Sugarless Cheesecake

Crust:

¾ c. graham cracker crumbs

3 Tbsp. butter, softened

Filling:

4 oz. light cream cheese, softened

½ pkg. sugar-free instant pudding (your favorite)

1 c. skim milk

Combine graham cracker crumbs and butter. Press into bottom and sides of 8" pie pan. Mix cream cheese, instant pudding mix and milk. Pour into crust. Chill before serving.

Hot Fudge Sundae Cake

1 c. flour

¾ c. sugar

2 Tbsp. cocoa

2 tsp. baking powder

¼ tsp. salt

½ c. milk

2 Tbsp. vegetable oil

1 tsp. vanilla

½ c. chopped nuts, optional

1 c. brown sugar

¼ c. cocoa

1¾ c. hot water

ice cream

Mix flour, sugar, cocoa, baking powder and salt in an ungreased pan. Mix in milk, vegetable oil and vanilla with fork until smooth. Stir in nuts. Spread evenly in pan. Mix 1 cup brown sugar and ¼ cup cocoa together. Sprinkle evenly on top of dough, do no mix. Pour hot water over top. Bake 40 minutes. Let set 10 minutes. Spoon on plates and top with ice cream. Spoon sauce over each serving. Leftovers may be reheated and served at next meal. To be served with ice cream. Delicious!

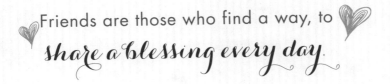

Friends are those who find a way, to *share a blessing every day*.

Almond-Peach Shortcake

¾ c. flour

1 Tbsp. sugar

1½ tsp. baking powder

½ tsp. salt

1 Tbsp. shortening

⅓ c. milk

½ Tbsp. margarine

¼ c. slivered almonds, or ½ tsp. almond extract

3 Tbsp. brown sugar

1½ c. unsweetened sliced peaches

Almond Whipped Cream:

½ c. whipping cream

1½ Tbsp. sugar

¼ tsp. almond extract

Heat oven to 400°. Grease an 8" pie plate. Mix flour, sugar, baking powder and salt. Cut in shortening. Spread in pan, brush with margarine. Sprinkle with almonds and brown sugar. Bake until golden brown, cut in wedges. Top each serving with almond whipped cream and peaches. Cream: Beat whipping cream with sugar and almond extract in chilled bowl until soft peaks form.

The secret of getting
ahead is getting started.

Topping for Cake

1 c. fresh or canned fruit (chopped)

1½ c. cold water or fruit juice

⅓ c. sugar

1 Tbsp. clear jel, heaping

4 oz. cream cheese

1 Tbsp. powdered sugar

½ c. Cool Whip

Mix first 4 ingredients together and bring to a boil. Cook until thickened. Cool. Meanwhile, mix cream cheese with powdered sugar. Add Cool Whip; mix well. Spread on a white or yellow cake. Top with fruit mixture. Refrigerate until ready to serve.

Jelly Roll

2 eggs, separated

½ c. sugar, divided

2½ Tbsp. water

½ tsp. vanilla

½ tsp. baking powder

⅛ tsp. salt

½ c. flour

Line a 9"x13" cookie sheet with wax paper. Beat together egg yolks with ¼ cup sugar, water and vanilla until light. Add baking powder, salt and flour, beat until thick. Set aside. Beat egg whites until soft peaks form. Add ¼ cup remaining sugar and beat until stiff peaks form. Fold egg yolks into egg whites. Spread evenly into pan and bake at 350° for 15 minutes. Let cool 5 minutes. Flip on heavy paper towel that has been dusted with powdered sugar. Peel off wax paper. Roll up, starting at short side. End with seam side under. When cool, unroll, peel off paper towel. Spread filling on jelly roll, and re-roll. When cold, wrap in cling wrap. Can be frozen. To freeze, it is best to wrap in freezer paper too. Filling: Cook a box of strawberry Danish according to directions. Cool completely before putting on jelly roll.

Angel Food Cake Rolls

4 c. egg whites (2 doz.)
3½ tsp. cream of tartar
½ tsp. salt
4 c. sugar, divided
2⅔ c. cake flour

Filling:
10 oz. cream cheese
2½ c. powdered sugar
20 oz. Cool Whip

Beat egg whites until foamy. Add cream of tartar and salt, beat until soft peaks form. Add 2 cups sugar, beat until stiff peaks form. Sift cake flour and 2 cups sugar together 3 times, then fold into egg whites slowly. Grease three 12"x17" pans with shortening, line with wax paper and spray with cooking spray. Divide batter evenly in 3 pans. Bake at 350° for 18–20 minutes. Let set in pan a few minutes then flip onto Bounty paper towels covered with powdered sugar sprinkled through a sifter. Make sure your paper towels are wider than the pan, and the thicker type of towels. Peel off wax paper. Roll up at the wide end, like a jelly roll. Let cool, seam side down. Then unwrap (peel off paper towels) spread with filling, and roll up again. To make filling: Beat ingredients well, and divide to approximately 2¼ cup filling per cake. Roll up and put seam-side-down. Cut each roll in half to make 6 cake rolls. Wrap and freeze. I wrap in cling wrap first, then freezer paper. It is easier to slice when frozen. If unexpected company comes, just take a cake roll out of the freezer. Enjoy! Make the fillings lavender, green and yellow for Easter; green and red for Christmas, with paste colorings. Or leave the filling white and add 2 tablespoons flavored Jell-O to the cake for color. For chocolate version: add ½ cup cocoa, 2¼ cup cake flour, instead of the 2⅔ cup cake flour.

Prize-Winning Sugar Cookies

½ c. brown sugar

½ c. sugar

½ c. butter

1 egg

½ c. milk

½ tsp. vanilla

2½ tsp. baking powder

1 tsp. baking soda

¼ tsp. salt

2½–3 c. flour

nuts, raisins, M&M's, chocolate chips, optional

Cream together sugars and butter. Add egg and cream some more. Add milk, vanilla, salt, baking powder and baking soda. Add flour, 1 cup at a time, mixing well. Drop on cookie sheets and bake. Don't over bake. Can be used for cutouts too. May need a little more flour. Roll out to approximately 12"–14". These cookies freeze well.

Mom's Molasses Cookies

¾ c. shortening

1 c. sugar

1 egg

¼ c. molasses

2 Tbsp. milk

1 tsp. vanilla

2½ c. flour

1½ tsp. baking soda

1 tsp. cinnamon

¾ tsp. salt

¾ tsp. nutmeg

In a bowl cream shortening and sugar. Beat in the egg, molasses, milk and vanilla. Combine flour, soda, cinnamon, salt and nutmeg; gradually add to creamed mixture. Cover and refrigerate 1 hour. Shape into 1" balls; roll in white sugar. Place on cookie sheets. Bake at 350° for 10–14 minutes or until tops crack and edges are slightly firm.

To flatten cookies on cookie sheet before baking, use bottom of a moistened glass, dipped in flour, or white sugar can be used if cookie will not be frosted.

Some flatten by themselves.

Peanut Butter Cookies

½ c. shortening

½ c. peanut butter

½ c. sugar

½ c. brown sugar

1 egg

1 ¼ c. flour

½ tsp. baking powder

¾ tsp. baking soda

¼ tsp. salt

Mix first five ingredients together. Sift remaining ingredients. Blend into
peanut butter mixture. Chill dough 1–2 hours. Shape into 1" balls. Place
on cookie sheet. Flatten with fork or potato masher dipped in flour. Bake at
350° until set, but not hard. Optional: roll balls in sugar, place on cookie
sheet. Do not dip potato masher in flour. Press a chocolate blossom into
each cookie as soon as you remove the cookies from the cookie sheet.
Cookies will then be called "Peanut Butter Blossoms."

Always test bake a
cookie. A foil pie pan
works good.

Peanut Butter Sandwich Cookies

1 c. butter

1 c. peanut butter

1 c. sugar

1 c. brown sugar

1 tsp. vanilla

3 eggs

4 c. all-purpose flour

2 tsp. baking powder

¼ tsp. salt

Filling:

½ c. peanut butter

1 tsp. vanilla

5-6 Tbsp. milk

3 c. powdered sugar

Cream together butter, peanut butter and sugars. Add vanilla and eggs, beating well. Add dry ingredients, mixing well. Shape into 1" balls. Place on ungreased baking sheets. Flatten with fork or potato masher. Bake at 375° for 5-6 minutes (don't over-bake). Remove from oven and leave on cookie sheet for 2–3 minutes before removing. They should be slightly brown on the bottom. Cool on wire racks. When cookies have cooled spread filling on half of the cookies and top each with another cookie. These freeze well.

Good friends know that love can
grow even in winter's snow.

Date Pinwheel Cookies

1 c. brown sugar

1 egg

⅓ c. lard or shortening

¼ tsp. salt

1½ tsp. baking powder

1 Tbsp. cream

1½ c. all-purpose flour

1 tsp. vanilla

Filling:

1½ c. chopped dates

⅓ c. water

¼ c. sugar

⅓ c. chopped nuts

Cook filling until dates are soft and spreadable, stirring constantly. Set aside to cool. Mix first three cookie ingredients well. Gradually add the rest, mixing well. Roll out in a rectangle about ½" thick. Spread filling on top. Roll up like a jelly roll, starting at long end. End with seam underneath. Put on a baking sheet and refrigerate overnight. Slice ½" thick. Place on cookie sheet and bake at 375° for 10–12 minutes. Don't over-bake. These cookies freeze well.

Cream Wafer Cookies

1 c. butter

2 c. brown sugar

4 eggs, beaten

2 tsp. vanilla

¼ c. sweet cream

1 Tbsp. baking soda

5½ c. all-purpose flour

Filling:

½ c. butter

¼ c. hot sweet cream

2 tsp. vanilla

4 c. powdered sugar

Cream butter, eggs and sugar. Gradually add the rest of ingredients, mixing well. Put dough through cookie press with the zig-zag grooves on top. Put strips lengthwise on cookie sheet, 3–4 to a sheet. Bake at 350° for 8–10 minutes, till they are just firm to touch. Use a metal spatula to slide underneath your cookie strip to cut loose. Slide the whole strip off the cookie sheet. When you are done baking the cookies, fill press with frosting. Flip half of cookie strips down-side-up. Add a strip of frosting, then another cookie strip on top. Cut to desired length. These cookies get better with age. They get very soft. Can be frozen several months, but ours don't usually last that long! If you want to make chocolate or strawberry cookies, add some Nesquik.

Use ⅛ cup or #40 ice cream
scoop for the drop cookies.

JUST YOU AND ME

Brown Sugar Cookies

¾ c. brown sugar

½ c. butter

1 egg

2 Tbsp. hot water

pinch of salt

½ tsp. baking soda

½ tsp. baking powder

1¾ c. flour

Cream sugar, butter and egg together. Add remaining ingredients. Drop on cookie sheets. Bake at 350°. I use a flat bottom glass dipped in flour and flatten each cookie a little bit before baking.

Buttermilk Cookies

1 c. brown sugar

1 egg

½ c. butter

½ c. buttermilk or sour milk

1½ tsp. baking powder

1 tsp. baking soda

½ tsp. vanilla

2 c. flour

Cream sugar, egg and butter together. Add buttermilk, baking soda, baking powder and vanilla. Mix well. Add flour and mix again. Drop by teaspoonfuls on cookie sheet and bake at 350° to desired doneness. You can add a little flour and chill for cut-outs. Frost with brown sugar icing. Yield: 3 dozen.

All-American Chocolate Chip Cookies

½ c. sugar

⅓ c. brown sugar

½ c. butter

½ c. peanut butter

½ tsp. vanilla

1 egg

¼ tsp. salt

1 tsp. baking soda

½ c. quick oats

1 c. flour

½ c. chocolate chips

Beat sugars, butter, peanut butter, vanilla and egg until well blended. Mix in salt, baking soda, oats and flour. Add chocolate chips; mix well. Drop on cookie sheets and bake at 350° for 10 minutes. Don't over bake.

Chocolate Chip Cookies

¾ c. margarine, softened

½ c. sugar

½ c. brown sugar

½ tsp. vanilla

1 egg

1 tsp. baking soda

½ tsp. salt

2 c. flour

2 c. semi-sweet chocolate chips

Mix margarine, sugars, vanilla and egg in bowl. Stir in baking soda, salt, flour and last, chocolate chips. Drop with teaspoon onto ungreased cookie sheet. Bake at 350° for 12–15 minutes or until light brown.

Filled Cookies

½ c. shortening

1 c. sugar (brown or white)

1 egg

1 tsp. vanilla

½ c. milk

3½ c. flour

1 tsp. baking soda

2 tsp. baking powder

Filling:

1 c. raisins or dates soaked in water then chopped

¾ c. sugar

1 c. water

1 Tbsp. clear jel

½ Tbsp. lemon juice

Pineapple Filling:

½ c. crushed pineapple, undrained

2 Tbsp. sugar

½ Tbsp. clear jel

Cook together filling ingredients until thick and clear. Cool. Mix cookie dough, roll out and cut in a 3" circle. Put 1 teaspoon filling in center. Top with another circle. Seal edges. Bake at 350° for about 20 minutes. Frost when cool. Punch out 1" circle of the top circle.

Mike Lizzie Cookies

(Fruit Bars or Raisin Bars)

This recipe dates back to the early 1900's. An all-time favorite among older people. Watch the smiles when you serve them.

⅔ c. sugar

⅓ c. butter

¼ c. Brer Rabbit molasses (I use mild flavor)

½ c. raisins

1 tsp. baking soda

1 egg, well-beaten

2 Tbsp. boiling water (raisin water, use to dissolve baking soda)

2 c. flour

1 egg, beaten

Barely cover raisins with water and cook until soft. Reserve 2 tablespoons raisin water. Drain raisins and cool. Mix sugar, flour and butter together. Work like pie dough. Add egg, molasses, raisins and baking soda (soda should be dissolved in 2 tablespoons raisin water). Mix well. Put on cookie sheet in strips, 2 per pan and length of pan. Press flat with spoon or your fingers. Beat 1 egg, brush on top just before you put pan in oven. Bake at 350° until done. Do not over bake. Cool partly, cut in 2" bars. Remove from pan and finish cooling.

Always pre-heat oven
before you start mixing
together your recipe.

Raisin Cookies

¼ c. butter

⅓ c. sugar

¼ tsp. vanilla

1 egg

¼ c. raisins

¾ c. all-purpose flour

pinch of salt

Cream butter and sugar, add vanilla and egg. Mix well. Add raisins, flour and salt. Stir until well blended. Form dough into a roll. Refrigerate until firm. Slice 3/8" thick. Bake on ungreased cookie sheet at 375° for 8–10 minutes or until light brown.

Soft Batch Cookies

¼ c. sugar

¼ c. brown sugar

¼ c. butter

1 egg

½ tsp. vanilla

½ tsp. baking soda

1 c. flour

½ c. chocolate chips

nuts, optional

Cream sugars and butter, add egg and vanilla. Mix well. Add baking soda, flour, chocolate chips and nuts. Mix will. Drop by teaspoonfuls onto cookie sheet. Bake at 350°. Do not over bake or they will harden.

Fresh Apple Bars

1½ c. sugar

¼ c. vegetable oil

2 eggs

½ tsp. baking soda

¼ tsp. cinnamon

½ tsp. salt

1 c. all-purpose flour

1 c. chopped apples

½ c. chopped nuts or raisins

Beat first 3 ingredients well. Add the rest and mix well. Spread mixture in a lightly-greased pan. Bake at 350° for 30 minutes.

Apple Bars

⅓ c. milk

1½ tsp. yeast

½ c. butter, softened

2 egg yolks

1¼ c. flour

2 c. apple pie filling

cinnamon or apple pie spice

Frosting:

2 Tbsp. butter

¾ c. powdered sugar

1 Tbsp. milk

Add yeast to lukewarm milk; stir with wire whisk. Add butter and beaten egg yolks. Mix. Add flour and mix well. Turn onto floured surface. Knead slightly. Divide dough in half. Press half of dough in a 9"x13" pan with your hands. Spread pie filling on top. Sprinkle with cinnamon or apple pie spice. Roll out other half of dough; lay on top of filling. Bake at 350° for 40-45 minutes. Cool before frosting. Cut in squares.

Marshmallow Brownies

⅓ c. butterscotch chips

2 Tbsp. butter

1 egg

¼ c. brown sugar, scant

⅓ tsp. vanilla

½ c. all-purpose flour

⅔ tsp. baking powder

pinch of salt

1 c. miniature marshmallows

½ c. semisweet chocolate chips

¼ c. chopped nuts

Over low heat melt butter and butterscotch chips; cool to lukewarm. In a mixing bowl beat egg, brown sugar and vanilla. Add butterscotch mixture, mix well. Add flour, baking powder and salt, mix well. Stir in marshmallows, chocolate chips and nuts. Spread in 8"x8" pan. Bake at 325° until done. Cool, cut in pieces. If you want more of a fudge taste, use milk chocolate chips instead of butterscotch.

Nut and Chip Bars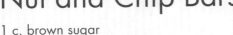

1 c. brown sugar

⅓ c. butter

1 egg

1 tsp. vanilla

½ tsp. baking powder

⅛ tsp. baking soda

1 c. flour

½ c. nuts

½ c. miniature chocolate chips

Cream sugar, butter and egg. Add vanilla, dry ingredients and nuts. Spread in a 9"x9" pan. Sprinkle chips on top. Bake at 350° for 25–30 minutes. Do not over bake.

Surprise Bars

1 c. sugar

⅔ c. vegetable oil

2 eggs, beaten

1 c. flour

1 tsp. baking soda

1 tsp. cinnamon

1½ c. grated carrots

½ c. nuts

½ c. raisins, optional

Frosting:

2 oz. cream cheese

3 Tbsp. butter

2 tsp. milk

2 tsp. vanilla

1½ c. powdered sugar

Cream sugar, vegetable oil and eggs. Add dry ingredients to egg mixture. Fold in carrots, raisins and nuts. Bake in a greased and floured 9"x13" pan, at 350° for 30–35 minutes. Frost when cool.

Cake with Creamy Orange Sauce

¼ c. Miracle Whip

¼ c. sour cream

2 tsp. brown sugar

2 tsp. orange juice

1 tsp. grated orange peel

pound cake or sponge cake

assorted fresh fruit

Mix all ingredients except cake and fruit. Refrigerate several hours or overnight. Layer sauce with pound cake and fruit in a clear glass bowl.

Sugar Glaze

(drizzle on cakes, muffins, cookies)

⅔ c. powdered sugar

3-4 Tbsp. milk

Stir together until all lumps are gone. If too thick, add a few more drops of milk for desired consistency. Yield: ¼ cup.

Brown Sugar Frosting

¼ c. butter

2 Tbsp. milk

½ c. brown sugar

1 c. powdered sugar

Put butter, milk and brown sugar in saucepan over low heat until melted. Bring to a boil. Cool. Add powdered sugar. If it gets too stiff, add a little water.

Frosting

½ c. Crisco or butter

2 c. powdered sugar

2 Tbsp. milk or hot water

vanilla or maple flavor, optional

food coloring, optional

Mix well. If too thick, thin by adding a few drops of liquid. Add a little powdered sugar if too thin. Butter will give frosting a hint of yellow. For creamier frosting, add more Crisco. This is enough frosting for 24 medium-size cookies. Can also be used for frosting cinnamon rolls.

Butter Cream Frosting

¼ c. Crisco

¼ c. butter

¼ tsp. vanilla

2 c. powdered sugar

1 Tbsp. milk

Cream Crisco and butter; add vanilla. Gradually add powdered sugar, beating well. Keep sides of bowl scraped. Add milk and beat until light and fluffy. Keep frosting covered when not in use. Can be stored in airtight container in refrigerator up to 2 weeks. If too thick, add 1–2 tablespoon corn syrup. For chocolate butter cream frosting: add ⅓ cup cocoa or a 1 ounce unsweetened chocolate square (melted) and an additional 1–2 tablespoon milk. Mix until well blended.

Each new day that passes by,
brings another chance to try.

Pies

Creamy Vanilla Crumb Pie

2 (9") unbaked pie crusts
8 oz. cream cheese
½ c. sugar
1 egg, beaten
½ tsp. salt
1 tsp. vanilla

Filling:
2 c. water
1 c. brown sugar
1 Tbsp. flour
1 c. Karo
1 egg, beaten
¼ c. clear jel
1 tsp. vanilla

Crumb Topping:
2 c. flour
½ c. brown sugar
½ c. butter, softened
1 tsp. baking powder
½ tsp. cream of tartar
½ tsp. cinnamon

Beat together cream cheese, sugar, egg, salt and vanilla. Spread in pie crusts. In medium saucepan, bring filling ingredients to a boil until thickened. Set aside to cool. Add vanilla. When cooled, pour over top of cream cheese mixture. Mix crumb topping until crumbly, spread over top of pie. Bake at 375° for 30–40 minutes.

Pear Pie

4 c. peeled and finely-sliced pears

⅓ c. sugar

1 Tbsp. clear jel

⅛ tsp. salt

1 unbaked pie shell

Crumbs:

½ c. shredded cheddar cheese

½ c. flour

¼ c. butter, melted

¼ c. sugar

¼ tsp. salt

Mix crumbs and set aside. Mix pear mixture and put in unbaked pie shell. Spread crumbs evenly over pears. Bake at 425° for 30–35 minutes. Cool 10 minutes. Serve warm. I like to sprinkle extra cheese over top after pie is baked. Very good!

All pies are baked using 9" round
pans unless otherwise stated.

Strawberry Pie

2 c. water

⅓ c. strawberry Danish

¼ c. sugar

3 Tbsp. clear jel

2 c. sliced strawberries, heaping

Cream Filling:

8 oz. cream cheese, softened

4 Tbsp. powdered sugar

8 oz. Cool Whip, thawed

Cook first 4 ingredients together until thickened, stirring constantly, over medium heat. Cool before adding sliced strawberries to the cooked glaze. Optional: put ½–¾ cup cream cheese in bottom of baked pie crust (use cream cheese in a tube from bulk food store). Or mix your own, using above filling ingredients. Put ¾ cup in baked pie crust. Refrigerate the rest for the next pie. Add a dab of topping on each piece of pie. Nobody can stay with only 1 strawberry pie.

Double Strawberry Yogurt Pie

2 c. fresh or frozen strawberries, quartered

¼ c. sugar

2 c. strawberry yogurt

1 pkg. unflavored gelatin

9" graham cracker crust

whipped topping or Cool Whip

sliced strawberries for garnish

Combine strawberries and sugar. Mash until chunky-smooth. Add yogurt. Mix well. Sprinkle gelatin over cold water in saucepan. Let stand 1 minute. Heat over low heat until dissolved. Add to yogurt mixture. Stir will. Pour in crust. Refrigerate until firm (4 hours). Garnish with topping and strawberries. If using frozen strawberries, use an extra 1½ teaspoon gelatin.

Sour Cream Blueberry Pie

1 egg
¾ c. sugar
2 Tbsp. flour
1 c. sour cream
½ tsp. vanilla
¼ tsp. salt
2 c. blueberries

  Crumbs:
3 Tbsp. flour
1½ Tbsp. butter
½ c. chopped nuts

Mix first 6 ingredients well. Add fruit and pour into unbaked pie shell. Bake at 400° for 25 minutes. Take from oven and add crumbs. Bake 10 minutes more.

Perma Flo keeps better than clear jel. A jar of pie filling will not thicken on the inside and will be runny on the outside. Fruit will not lose its flavor.

Sour Cream Rhubarb Pie

1 c. chopped rhubarb
¾ c. water
1 Tbsp. clear jel
2 Tbsp. strawberry or cherry Jell-O
¼ c. sugar

Filling:
½ c. sugar
¾ c. sour cream
4 oz. cream cheese
¼ tsp. salt
4 tsp. flour

Crumbs:
½ c. flour
¼ c. sugar
2 Tbsp. butter

Put first five ingredients in a saucepan. Bring to a boil, stirring constantly. Cook until thickened. Set side. Cool completely. Meanwhile mix the filling. Mix the crumbs. When the rhubarb sauce is cold, pour into unbaked pie crust. Top with filling, be sure to seal the edges to the pie crust. Put crumbs on top. Bake at 350° for 45 minutes. Tastes like spring in the middle of the winter.

Cook fresh rhubarb for sauce with whatever water clings to the stalks after washing. Don't add more water. Add sugar to taste.

Mince Pie

1 egg, beaten
1 c. sugar
½ c. molasses
¼ c. butter
½ tsp. cinnamon
½ tsp. allspice
½ tsp. cloves
1 c. water
¼ c. vinegar
½ c. raisins
½ c. toasted bread crumbs

Mix all together, let set 5 minutes. Pour into unbaked pie shell. Bake at 350° for 45 minutes or until golden brown and almost set in center.

Pecan Pie

4 eggs, beaten
¾ c. brown sugar
2 Tbsp. flour
1½ c. Karo
½ tsp. salt
¼ c. water
3 Tbsp. butter, melted
1 c. pecans, chopped

Mix flour and nuts, set aside. Mix beaten eggs, sugar, Karo, salt, and water together. Add nuts and flour, last add melted butter, blend well. Pour into unbaked pie shell. Bake at 350° for 45-50 minutes until center is almost set.

Eggnog Pie

1 tsp. unflavored gelatin

1 Tbsp. cold water

1 c. milk

½ c. sugar

2 Tbsp. clear jel

½ tsp. salt

3 egg yolks, beaten

1 Tbsp. butter

1 Tbsp. vanilla

1 c. whipping cream

1½ c. Cool Whip

Soak gelatin in cold water. In a saucepan, bring to a boil and cook until thickened—milk, sugar, clear jel, salt and egg yolks. Remove from heat, add butter and gelatin. Set aside to cool. Meanwhile whip the whipping cream. Fold into cooled filling, and pour into baked pie crust. Refrigerate. Put Cool Whip on top before serving. This is very good to divide into 2 pans and fill with fresh strawberry pie filling. Even for 2 pies, they will be gone before you realize what happened.

Pumpkin Pie

1½ c. milk

3 eggs

1 c. sugar

½ c. pumpkin

1 tsp. pumpkin pie spice

1 Tbsp. flour

Heat milk to lukewarm. Separate 2 of the eggs. Beat 2 egg whites until stiff. Set aside. Cream egg yolks, remaining egg and sugar; add pumpkin, spice and flour. Add warm milk and mix well. Add egg whites and fold in. Pour into unbaked pie crust. Bake at 350° for 45 minutes.

Creamy Pumpkin Pie

Crust:

½ c. flour

½ c. wheat flour

¼ c. brown sugar

¼ c. butter

¼ c. pumpkin (from can used in the filling)

1 c. quick oats

¼ c. walnuts

Filling:

8 oz. cream cheese, softened

½ c. sugar

1 (15 oz.) can pumpkin

1 tsp. cinnamon

⅛ tsp. nutmeg

¼ tsp. salt

3 eggs

1 tsp. vanilla

Mix crust ingredients, put in pie pan and bake at 350° for 15 minutes. Cool. Filling: Mix cream cheese, sugar, pumpkin and spices until creamy; add eggs and vanilla. Beat until smooth. Pour into cooled crust. Bake 35–40 minutes. Refrigerate until ready to serve.

When you thicken with clear jel or Perma Flo, it will stay however thick you make it. If you thicken with flour, it will become a little thicker when it cools.

Custard Pie

1 c. sugar, (or ½ c. white sugar and ½ c. brown sugar)
3 eggs, separated
pinch of salt
1 Tbsp. flour
1½ c. milk
vanilla

Cream together sugar, egg yolks and salt. Add flour. Add milk and heat to lukewarm. Add vanilla. Beat egg whites until stiff peaks form. Fold into milk mixture. Pour into unbaked pie shell. Bake at 350° for 45 minutes or until center is almost set. For pumpkin pie: Omit vanilla and add 1 teaspoon pumpkin pie spice and ⅓ cup pumpkin.

Custard Pie

2 eggs, (1 egg, separated)
1 tsp. vanilla
1 Tbsp. flour
½ can Eagle Brand milk
2 c. milk

Combine eggs, vanilla, flour and Eagle Brand milk. Mix well. Add milk, then beaten egg white. Bake at 350° for 40–45 minutes, until center is almost set.

Bake custard, pumpkin and pecan pies until nice and brown but so that the center is not set (leave a little shaky).

Raisin Cream Pie

1 c. cooked raisins
2 c. milk
½ c. brown sugar
½ c. sugar
2 egg yolks, beaten
6 Tbsp. flour
1 Tbsp. butter

Put enough water in saucepan to cover raisins. Simmer until water is almost gone. Put all other ingredients together, except butter. Cook until thick, stirring constantly. Then add cooked raisins and butter. Stir until butter is melted. When cold, put in baked pie crust. Garnish with whipped topping.

Pumpkin Pecan Pie

Pumpkin Layer:
1 egg, beaten
1 c. pumpkin
⅓ c. sugar
1 tsp. pumpkin pie spice

Pecan Layer:
⅔ c. Karo
2 eggs, beaten
½ c. sugar
3 Tbsp. butter
½ tsp. vanilla
1 c. pecan halves or pieces

Combine pie ingredients. Spread in the bottom of an unbaked pie shell. Combine pecan layer and mix well. Spoon over pumpkin layer. Bake at 350° for 50 minutes or until filling is set.

Mock Pecan Pie

½ c. sugar

¼ c. butter, melted

1 tsp. vanilla

¼ tsp. salt

3 eggs

1 c. Karo

1 c. oatmeal

Mix in order given. Pour into unbaked pie shell. Bake at 350° for 45 minutes or until center is almost set.

Lemon Cloud Pie

4 oz. Cool Whip

1 can Eagle Brand milk

½ c. ReaLemon

Mix well and pour into a baked pie shell. Garnish with whipped topping.

Lemon Pie

3 egg yolks

1¼ c. sugar

3½ Tbsp. clear jel

¼ c. ReaLemon

½ c. water

Cool Whip

Beat egg yolks and add the rest of the ingredients, except Cool Whip in a saucepan and cook until thickened. Cool and pour into a baked pie shell. Cool Whip may be added for a milder taste. Put a dab of Cool Whip on each piece before serving, or beat egg whites to stiff peaks, and add 1 teaspoon sugar. Beat in. Put on top of pie and put in broiler until peaks are brown.

Apple Pie Crumbs

½ c. flour

½ c. Bisquick

¼ c. butter, softened

¼ c. brown sugar

Mix all together until crumbly. Can be made the day before. Fill a pre-baked crust with apple pie filling. Spread crumbs on top. Bake at 350° until crumbs are brown.

Apple Cream Pie

⅔ c. sugar

2 Tbsp. flour

⅛ tsp. salt

1 c. sour cream

1 egg, slightly beaten

1 tsp. vanilla

2 c. finely-chopped apples

Crumbs:

¼ c. butter

½ c. flour

⅓ c. sugar

1 tsp. cinnamon

Combine sugar, flour and salt. Add sour cream, egg, and vanilla and beat until smooth. Add chopped apples and pour into unbaked pie crust. Mix crumbs and put on top. Bake at 425° for 25 minutes.

Pies

Dutch Apple Pie

3 c. shredded apples

½ tsp. cinnamon

¼ c. brown sugar

2 Tbsp. flour

#1 Crumbs:

¾ c. flour

½ c. brown sugar

2 Tbsp. butter

#2 Crumbs:

½ c. oatmeal

½ c. flour

⅛ tsp. baking soda

½ c. brown sugar

⅛ tsp. baking powder

Crumbs can be made ahead of time. Mix together like pie dough, until you have fine crumbs. Set aside. Crumbs can be put in a tight container if you don't use them all. Use within a week or two. Roll out pie crust and put in pie pan. Set aside. Peel, core and shred apples. Mix in other 3 ingredients. Put in pie pan, with crumbs on top. Make sure all apples are covered. Bake at 350° for 35–45 minutes, until crumbs are golden brown. A slice of hot apple pie with cold milk, is a meal by itself. I prefer Yellow Delicious or Golden Delicious apples. Red Delicious turn brown too quickly and have too much juice.

JUST YOU AND ME

Fresh Fruit Pie

1 ¾ c. unsweetened flaked coconut

2 egg whites, beaten until foamy

1 (8.25 oz.) can unsweetened crushed pineapple with juice

1 Tbsp. clear jel

2 bananas, sliced in orange juice and drained

fresh peaches or strawberries, sliced

additional fruit slices and coconut to garnish

Preheat oven to 325°. Toss coconut and egg whites together; press into bottom and sides of pie pan. Bake 10 minutes. Cool. Mix pineapple and clear jel, cook until thickened. Cool. Layer bananas, pineapple mixture and fresh fruit into shell. Dab each piece of pie with topping and top with a slice of peach or strawberry. Chill 3 hours. Great for sugar-conscious people. Be creative, decorate to your heart's content. Small strawberries work great, or raspberries, blueberries, etc.

Peanut Butter Pie

8 oz. cream cheese

¾ c. powdered sugar

⅓ c. peanut butter

2 tsp. milk

1 tsp. vanilla

8 oz. Cool Whip

1 pie crust or graham cracker crust

Combine cream cheese, powdered sugar, peanut butter, milk and vanilla. Beat until smooth. Fold in Cool Whip. Pour in crust. Sprinkle crushed graham cracker crumbs on top. Freeze 2 hours or until firm.

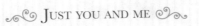

JUST YOU AND ME

Sunshine Orange Mousse Pie

1 Tbsp. unflavored gelatin

¼ c. cold water

1 c. whipping cream (heat to boiling)

8 oz. cream cheese, softened

6 oz. frozen orange juice concentrate

¾ c. powdered sugar

1½ tsp. vanilla

9" graham cracker crust

Sprinkle gelatin over cold water. Let set 1 minute. Add cream and stir until gelatin is dissolved. Add cream cheese, juice concentrate, sugar and vanilla. Stir until blended. Chill until slightly thickened, pour into crust. Chill. Garnish with orange slices or fresh fruit.

Butterscotch Pie

1½ c. brown sugar

2 Tbsp. butter

5 Tbsp. whipping cream

2 eggs

4 Tbsp. flour

Boil together 5 minutes. Set off of heat. Meanwhile, cream together with beaters:

2 c. milk

2 Tbsp. clear jell

Add to first ingredients, stirring constantly with spatula. Bring to a boil. Cook slightly and pour into a baked pie shell. Refrigerate until ready to serve.

Basic Cream Pie Filling

3 eggs, separated
2½ c. milk
½ c. sugar
½ c. brown sugar
pinch of salt
¼ c. clear jel
¼ c. flour

In a saucepan, beat egg yolks, add milk, sugars, salt, clear jel and flour. Stir until lumps are gone. Over low heat, cook until thickened, stirring constantly. Set aside. Beat egg whites into very stiff peaks. Fold into cooked mixture. Use for coconut cream, peanut butter cream, and graham cracker pudding. Spoon over a dish of fresh strawberries or peaches. For coconut pie: Put some coconut in baked pie crust, fill with cooked filling. Sprinkle some toasted coconut on top. Refrigerate until ready to serve. For peanut butter pie: Mix ¾ cup peanut butter with enough powdered sugar until crumbly. Put desired amount of crumbs in baked pie shell. Fill with cooked filling, and a thin layer of Cool Whip. Put another layer of peanut butter crumbs on top. Refrigerate until ready to serve. If filling is too rich and thick, you can stir in some Cool Whip.

Chess Pie

9 Tbsp. butter
1 c. sugar
3 Tbsp. flour
pinch of salt
3 eggs
Add:
1 c. chopped nuts
1 c. raisins
¼ tsp. vanilla

Cream eggs, sugar, butter. Add vanilla, salt, flour. Mix well and add nuts and raisins. Pour into unbaked pie shell and bake at 350° for 40-45 min.

Pie Pastry

5 lb. Gold Medal flour (All Purpose)
1 (3 lb.) can butter Crisco
½ c. sugar
2 Tbsp. salt

Mix together; store in an air-tight bowl in a cool, dry place. It will keep a long time. I use 1 cup crumbs to 1 ounce + 1 Tbsp. water. (6 cups crumbs to 1 cup cold water) 1 cup crumbs = 1 pie crust.

Push Pastry

1½ c. flour
1 Tbsp. sugar
1 tsp. salt
2 Tbsp. milk
½ c. vegetable or olive oil

Mix together and press in pie pan.

Graham Cracker Crust

6 graham crackers
3 Tbsp. butter, melted
1 Tbsp. sugar

Melt butter, set aside. Crush crackers extra fine, and put in pie pan. Add sugar and melted butter. Mix with a fork until crackers are coated with butter. Use a fork and press cracker crumbs in the bottom and side of pan. Bake at 350° for 5 minutes. Cool before filling. Can be made a day or so ahead.

Ice Cream
& Toppings

Edible Chocolate Cups

8 oz. chocolate

1 Tbsp. shortening

12 cupcake papers

ice cream or sherbet

chocolate curls, citrus curls or fresh fruit to garnish

Melt chocolate (You can use semisweet chocolate, milk chocolate or white chocolate) and shortening. Stir until smooth. Put cupcake papers in pan. Using a clean brush, spread about 2 teaspoons melted chocolate onto bottom and up the sides of each cup. Chill until firm, about 10 minutes, reserving any extra chocolate. Re-melt extra chocolate and reinforce any weak spots inside the cups (especially near the top). Cups can be made 2 days ahead. Refrigerate. Cover loosely with plastic wrap. Loosen top edge of paper and gently peel away from chocolate cup. Can be filled with a scoop of ice cream, 2 hours ahead of serving time and kept in freezer. Garnish immediately before serving. Good idea to make a few extra in case you break a bowl. Good luck!

Maple Ice Cream

2 Tbsp. plain gelatin

½ c. cold water

1¼ c. milk

1 egg

½ c. maple syrup

¼ c. sweet cream

½ tsp. maple flavoring

pinch of salt

Soak gelatin in cold water for 2–5 minutes. Heat milk, mix gelatin into hot milk, stir until dissolved. Separate egg and beat yolk. Add milk, maple syrup, cream, gelatin mixture, flavoring and salt. Beat egg white to stiff peaks. Beat into ice cream mixture. Pour in freezer can. Let set about 1 hour. Leaving it set makes smoother ice cream. Freeze according to directions. Yield: 1 quart ice cream.

Homemade Ice Cream

1 (3.4 oz.) instant pudding, any flavor
5 c. cold milk
½ c. brown sugar
¼ c. Karo

In a mixing bowl, mix ingredients thoroughly, approximately ¾ cup mix to a freezer. Yield: 8 freezers full. Freeze in White Mountain Ice Cream Freezer (junior size). Freeze according to manufacturer's instructions. Freeze extras in small containers for later. Or use a ½ gallon freezer. Note: Snow can be used instead of ice. Use plenty of salt. Approximately 10–15 minutes of cranking per freezer. The junior size freezer is a project for the grandchildren at the kitchen sink. Have the oldest ones mix together the ice cream ingredients, while the younger ones take a big bowl and spoon and go gather snow.

Simply Delicious Homemade Ice Cream

8 c. milk
1 (3.4 oz.) instant pudding mix, any flavor
1 c. whipping cream or half-and-half
1 (14 oz.) can sweetened condensed milk

Mix well and freeze in ice cream freezer according to manufacturer's instructions. This will fill a one gallon freezer by the time it is frozen.

Hot Fudge Sauce

1 c. chocolate Nesquik
¼ c. milk
¼ c. Karo
3 Tbsp. butter

In a saucepan, combine Nesquik, milk and Karo. Bring to a full boil, stirring constantly. Remove from heat, add butter. Serve warm or cool over ice cream or cake. Use Hot Fudge Sundae Cake in cake section.

Peach Sauce for Ice Cream

¾ c. peach juice

⅓ c. sugar

4 tsp. clear jel

¼ tsp. vanilla

½ c. chopped peaches

In a saucepan mix sugar and clear jel. Slowly add peach juice. Put on medium heat, add vanilla and chopped peaches. Bring to a boil, stirring constantly. Simmer until thick. Serve hot or cold over ice cream. Refrigerate leftover sauce.

Topping for Ice Cream

Two fresh peaches, peeled, pitted and chopped. Add sugar to your taste. Let set until sugar is melted. Serve over ice cream.

Strawberry Topping for Ice Cream

Wash, hull and drain strawberries. Chop or mash strawberries. Add desired amount of sugar. Stir until sugar is dissolved. Put in pint freezer boxes, leaving ¾" space at the top and freeze. When ready to serve thaw to your liking and serve over ice cream.

Once the ship has sunk, everyone knows how it might have been saved.

Candies & Snacks

Caramels

¼ c. butter

½ c. brown sugar, firmly packed

pinch of salt

¼ c. light corn syrup

3½ oz. or ¼ can sweetened condensed milk

¼ tsp. vanilla

Melt butter in a saucepan; stir in brown sugar and salt. Add corn syrup and mix well. Add sweetened condensed milk, stirring constantly. Continue stirring and cook over medium heat to 245°–250°. Remove from heat and stir in vanilla. Pour into a greased pan. Cool, cut in squares and wrap in wax paper. Yield: approximately 25 pieces.

Million Dollar Fudge

1 c. chopped walnuts

12 oz. chocolate chips

1 (10.75 oz.) chocolate bar

1 pt. marshmallow creme

1 tsp. vanilla

4 c. sugar

1 can evaporated milk

In a large mixing bowl, mix chopped nuts, chocolate chips, chocolate bar (broken in small pieces), marshmallow creme and vanilla. In saucepan, heat sugar and evaporated milk and bring to a boil. Boil 4 minutes, stirring constantly. Pour hot mixture over contents in bowl. Stir until melted, then pour in buttered pans. When set, cut in squares. I poured it in ½ cup containers with lids, and used it for Christmas gifts. Makes approximately 5 pounds.

Hard Tack

3¾ c. sugar

1½ c. light corn syrup

1 c. water

flavoring and food coloring

Mix sugar, corn syrup and water in a large saucepan until sugar is dissolved. Boil without stirring until temperature reaches 310° on candy thermometer. Remove from heat. Stir in flavoring and food coloring. Meanwhile sprinkle powdered sugar on cookie sheet. Pour into pan. Cool. Break into pieces.

Peanut Brittle

3 c. sugar

1¾ c. light corn syrup

1 c. water

3 c. raw peanuts

2 Tbsp. butter

1 tsp. salt

2½ tsp. baking soda

Cook sugar, corn syrup and water in a large saucepan. Heat to 240°. Add peanuts. Cook to 295°, stirring constantly. Remove from heat, add butter and stir until dissolved. Add salt and soda, stirring vigorously. Mixture will foam. Pour onto a well buttered cookie sheet and spread as thin as possible. Break into pieces when cool.

It's the counterfeit of happiness

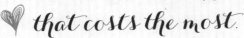

that costs the most.

Toffee

1 c. sugar

¾ c. margarine

¼ c. water

1 Tbsp. corn syrup

dipping chocolate

Mix sugar, margarine, water and corn syrup in a saucepan, stirring until sugar is melted. Cook slowly to 300°. Stir constantly to keep from scorching. This step will take some time. Pour into a buttered 8-inch square pan. When candy is cool, spread with melted dipping chocolate. When cold, break into pieces.

Mints

1 oz. cream cheese, room temperature

food coloring and flavoring, a few drops each

½ c. powdered sugar

sugar

candy molds

Mix cream cheese with coloring and flavoring until smooth. Work in powdered sugar and knead with hands to form a dough. Roll in small balls and roll each in white sugar. Once you have rolled the mint in sugar, do not re-shape—the mint will taste grainy if you do. Press mint into mold and release immediately. Store in covered container until ready to use. Do not cover with plastic wrap or the sugar will dissolve.

Peanut Clusters

Use equal amounts of coating chocolate and roasted peanuts. Melt chocolate in double boiler over warm water (not boiling). Stir in peanuts. Drop by spoonfuls on waxed paper. Cool. Try a variation: raisins, broken pretzels, cashews, pecans, walnuts. Make some with chocolate coating and some with white coating.

Dipped Pretzels

Melt chocolate. Take small stick pretzels and dip into chocolate, just so your finger doesn't touch melted chocolate. Place dipped pretzels on wax paper to cool. (Looks like drumsticks.) Store in tight container until ready to serve.

Mocha Fudge

1 Tbsp. butter
⅓ c. Carnation evaporated milk
¾ c. sugar
¼ tsp. salt
1 c. miniature marshmallows
½ c. semisweet chocolate chips
¼ c. butterscotch chips
½ Tbsp. instant coffee
½ tsp. vanilla
¼ c. chopped nuts

Combine butter, milk, sugar and salt in a saucepan over medium heat. Bring to a boil. Cook 4–5 minutes, stirring constantly. Remove from heat. Stir in marshmallows, chocolate and butterscotch chips, coffee, vanilla and nuts. Stir until marshmallows melt. Pour into 8" square pan. Garnish with pecan or walnut halves. Cool, cut in squares. For chocolate fudge: substitute ¼ c. chocolate chips for butterscotch chips; omit instant coffee.

Mistakes are part of the dues
one pays for a full life.

Caramel Corn

2 qt. popped corn
2 Tbsp. Karo
½ c. brown sugar
¼ c. butter
pinch of salt
pinch of baking soda
drop of vanilla

Large Quantity Recipe:
8 qt. popped corn
½ c. Karo
2 c. brown sugar
1 c. butter
1 tsp. salt
½ tsp. baking soda
1 tsp. vanilla

Boil Karo, sugar, butter and salt for 5 minutes. Remove from heat; add soda and vanilla. Pour over popcorn and mix well. Bake in a 6 quart stainless steel mixing bowl. Bake at 250° for 1 hour. Stir every 15 minutes. I like to use the big recipe and give as gifts. Or put in ½ gallon jars to set around at Christmas time. Put a piece of Christmas fabric on top and tie with a ribbon.

Party Mix

¼ c. butter or Wesson oil

1 Tbsp. Worcestershire sauce

½ tsp. onion salt

½ tsp. garlic salt

¾ tsp. seasoned salt

1 c. Corn Chex

1 c. Wheat Chex

1 c. Rice Chex

1 c. Fruit Loops

1 c. Honey Comb

1 c. mini pretzel twists

¾ c. mixed nuts

¾ c. cashews

In saucepan melt butter and add Worcestershire sauce and salts. Pour over cereals, nuts and pretzels in a large mixing bowl. Stir until well-coated. Bake 2 hours at 200°, stirring every 30 minutes. Pour on paper towels to cool. Store in airtight container. If you want a little bigger batch make cups heaping full when measuring. Note: When using Wesson oil mix together cold.

In youth we learn;
in age we understand.

Party Mix (Large Batch)

4 c. vegetable oil

6 Tbsp. Worcestershire sauce

3 Tbsp. onion powder

3 Tbsp. garlic salt

3 Tbsp. seasoned salt

12 c. (15 oz. box) Corn Chex

12 c. (16 oz. box) Wheat Chex

16 c. (15 oz. box) Rice Chex

16 c. (1½ lb.) Trix or Fruit Loops

12 c. (16 oz.) Honey Comb

10 c. (16 oz.) small pretzels

1–2 lb. mixed nuts

1–2 lb. cashews

Mix Worcestershire sauce with onion powder, garlic salt and seasoned salt. Add vegetable oil. Mix well. Put ½ of cereals in a large storage container. Pour ½ of seasonings, stirring at all times, so you don't get just the oil. Add last of cereal, then rest of seasonings. Try to spread all over. Close container and toss to make sure all is coated. Put in 13 quart mixing bowls and bake in the oven at 200° for 2 hours, stirring every 30 minutes. I like to make this and use as Christmas gifts or simply pass it out to friends.

Who's Old?

"To me, old age is always
fifteen years older than I am."

Party Mix

1 c. Honey Comb

1 c. Rice Chex

1 c. pretzels

1 c. Bugles

1 c. Ritz Bits crackers

1 tsp. seasoned salt

4 Tbsp. butter, melted

1 Tbsp. Worcestershire sauce

Melt butter and add seasonings. Pour over cereals and mix until well-coated. Pour in a pan and bake at 200° for 1 hour. Stir every 15 minutes.

Spicy Party Mix

2 Tbsp. butter

2 tsp. Worcestershire sauce

¾ tsp. seasoned salt

2 tsp. red pepper sauce

1 c. Corn Chex

1 c. Wheat Chex

1 c. Rice Chex

1 c. mixed nuts

1 c. alphabet pretzels

Heat oven to 200°. Melt butter, stir in seasonings. Pour over dry ingredients, stir until well-coated. Bake 1 hour, stirring every 15 minutes. Spread on paper towels to cool. Store in an airtight container.

Snack Crackers

¼ lb. saltine or Ritz crackers

¼ c. vegetable oil

1½ tsp. sour cream and onion powder

Mix onion powder and vegetable oil together. Pour over crackers and toss until well coated. Bake at 250° for 15–20 minutes.

Snack Crackers

2 pkg. Ritz crackers

¼ c. vegetable oil

1 Tbsp. Hidden Valley Ranch powder mix

¼ tsp. dill weed

⅛ tsp. garlic salt

Mix all ingredients together except crackers. Pour liquid over crackers in a sealable bowl. Put lid on and toss until well coated. Let set 1 hour. Keep leftovers in a tightly sealed container.

Puppy Chow

½ c. chocolate chips

⅓ c. peanut butter

2 Tbsp. butter

4 c. Crispix

¾ c. powdered sugar

Melt first three ingredients. Place cereal in bowl and pour melted syrup over cereal. Stir until well coated; cool. Sprinkle with powdered sugar and toss until coated. Store in a tight container.

Peanut Butter Balls

¼ c. butter

½ c. peanut butter

¼ c. light corn syrup

2–2½ c. powdered sugar

Mix first 3 ingredients together, add powdered sugar, 1 cup at a time. Roll into ¾ inch balls and coat with dipping chocolate.

Apple Snack

Cut an apple in half. Core and peel. Fill hole with crunchy peanut butter right out of the jar. Serve and watch the smiles.

Rice Krispie Squares

2 Tbsp. butter

2 c. miniature marshmallows

2½ c. Rice Krispies

Melt butter in a saucepan over low heat. Add marshmallows, stir until melted and well blended. Remove from heat, add Rice Krispies. Stir until coated. Press in pan. Cool. Cut in squares.

Ritz Cookie Crackers

1 pkg. Ritz cookies
½ can Eagle Brand milk
½ c. chopped dates
½ c. chopped nuts

Frosting:
1½ oz. cream cheese
½ c. powdered sugar
¼ tsp. vanilla

Heat milk and dates until thick, stirring constantly. Add nuts. Spread 1 teaspoon mix on crackers. Bake at 250° for 5 minutes. Cool. Frost each cracker.

Patio Cheesecake

12 Ritz crackers
cream cheese, softened
powdered sugar

Mix cream cheese and powdered sugar together. Spread on Ritz crackers and top with fresh fruit pieces.

Finger Jell-O

½ c. Jell-O, any flavor
1 c. boiling water

Put Jell-O in a bowl, add boiling water. Stir until Jell-O is dissolved. Pour in a pan. Let set until cold. Cut in squares or use small cookie cutters of different shapes. Scraps can be melted and used again. Refrigerate until ready to serve. Do several flavors to make a colorful plate. A project the grandchildren enjoy.

Finger Jell-O

2 Tbsp. unflavored gelatin

1 c. cold water

½ c. Jell-O, any flavor

2 Tbsp. sugar

1¼ c. boiling water

Put gelatin in cold water, set aside. Put Jell-O and sugar in a bowl. Add 1¼ cups boiling water. Add gelatin and stir until everything is dissolved. Add ½ cup cold water. Pour in pan and untill firm. Cut in squares or use cookie cutters. Refrigerate.

Banana Roll-up

1 flour tortilla

peanut butter

mini chocolate chips

1 banana or 1 shredded apple

Spread a tortilla with peanut butter, then sprinkle with chocolate chips. Wrap around the banana. Slice into ½" slices. Serve with a smile. Nutritious snack to serve at your next tea party.

Just you and me

Canning & Freezing

Fruit Filling for Cobblers

18 c. juice (black raspberry)

4 c. sugar

1¾ c. Perma Flo

½ c. raspberry Danish

1 pkg. raspberry Kool-Aid

Mix all ingredients together. Bring to a boil, stirring constantly until thickened. Spoon into jars. Cold pack 10 minutes. Makes approximately 10 quart. Our favorite flavor is elderberry. The cobbler recipe is found in the Desserts section.

Apple Pie Filling to Can

9 c. water

9 c. apple juice

3 c. Perma Flo

6½ c. sugar

5–10 lb. shredded apples or 25 apples, a total
    of 36 cups shredded apples

cinnamon or apple pie spice (I used 2 tsp. apple pie spice)

Put water, juice, Perma Flo and sugar in a large stockpot or canner. Bring to a boil, stirring continuously. Cook until thick and clear. Divide it into two - 12 quart mixing bowls. Add spice. Mix well. Peel and shred apples. Add to cooked filling. The apples and spice are to be divided among the 2 bowls. More or less apples can be added to suit your taste. Fill jars only ¾ full. Cold pack 10 minutes; let set another 10 minutes before you take jars out of water. I like to use Golden Delicious apples. Makes approximately 11 quart. Can also be used for apple crisp. Apple crisp recipe can be found in Desserts.

Fillings can be used to make puddings too. When cooking filling, it's thick enough if you can put a spoonful on a plate, it stays in a heap and doesn't run all over the plate.

Apple Pie Filling to Can

28 c. shredded apples

5 c. sugar

1 c. brown sugar

1¾ c. Perma Flo

8 c. water

1 Tbsp. lemon juice

2½ tsp. apple pie spice

Put everything except apples in a large stockpot or canner. Cook until thickened and clear. Pour in a 12 quart stainless steel bowl. Add shredded apples. Mix well. Fill jars ¾ full and cold pack 10 minutes. Let set 10 minutes before you take jars out of canner.

Grape or Raspberry Pie Filling

18 c. juice

4 c. sugar

2½ c. Perma Flo

For Raspberry add:

½ c. raspberry Danish

1 pkt. raspberry Kool-Aid

For Grape add:

¼ c. grape Jell-O

1 pkt. grape Kool-Aid

Mix all your ingredients together. Bring to a boil, stirring constantly, until thickened. Spoon into jars. Cold pack 10 minutes. Makes approximately 5 quart. Any of these fruit pie fillings can be used to make the cream cheese pie filling dessert found in Desserts section.

Perma Flo can be used in anything you would use clear jel.

Strawberry Pie Filling

18 c. water

6 c. sugar

1 pkg. strawberry Kool-Aid

3 c. Perma Flo

1½ c. strawberry Danish

4½–5 qt . sliced strawberries

Cook filling ingredients (except strawberries) together until thick. Cool, add strawberries. I like small strawberries, so I need to cut them only once. Cold pack 8 minutes. Let set another 10 minutes, take out of canner. Makes approximately 10 quart. Put a layer of eggnog filling in pre-baked pie crust. Put strawberry filling on top. Dab with Cool Whip. Refrigerate 2–3 hours. Serve cold. Eggnog filling can be found in Pie section.

Sour Cherry Pie Filling

5 lb. frozen, pitted sour cherries (thaw and drain overnight)

24 c. water including cherry juice

5 c. sugar

3 c. Perma Flo

¼ c. cherry Jell-O

1 pkg. cherry Kool-Aid

red coloring, optional

Mix all together in canner or stock pot except cherries. Cook until thick, stirring constantly. Last add cherries. Make sure you have cherries all the way to the bottom. Spoon in jars and cold pack 8 minutes. Let set another 15 minutes. If you freeze your own cherries; 5 pounds cherries, 1 pound sugar.

I like to cook my pie fillings and soups in a heavy stainless steel canner (20 quart). Use a long-handled heavy stainless steel spatula for stirring. Much easier to keep it from scorching on the bottom.

Peach Pie Filling

(Using canned peaches)

10 qt. peaches with juice

5 qt. water

1 c. peach Danish

1 pkg. orange Kool-Aid

5 c. sugar

4 c. Perma Flo

Put canned peaches in stockpot and mash or chop them. Add rest of ingredients, bring to a boil and cook until thickened, stirring constantly. If not thick enough mix ½ cup Perma Flo with enough water to make it pourable. Add slowly, stirring until thick enough. If too thick, add water or peach juice. You can add 2–3 cans crushed pineapple and same amount water for peach-pineapple pie filling.

Peach Pie Filling

(using fresh peaches)

6 qt. sliced peaches

3 c. pineapple juice

4 c. water

7 c. sugar

2 c. Perma Flo

2/3 c. boxes peach Jell-O

Mix pineapple juice, water, sugar and Perma Flo together in 20 quart canner. Bring to a boil, stirring constantly until thickened, add Jell-O. Mix well, then add peaches. Spoon in jars. Cold pack 10 minutes. Let set another 10 minutes. Take out of canner.

Fluff your Perma Flo when you measure, rather than pack it. It is easier to add more, than take out, if it is too thick.

Pears

Cut pear halves in 6 pieces. Add green coloring to a pitcher full of syrup. In another pitcher of syrup, add red coloring. Fill your jars with red or green, and some with the regular syrup. Looks nice on pantry shelf. Grandchildren take a special liking to the colored ones. I like to make the red syrup with the cinnamon candy discs. You need to preheat the syrup to melt the candy. Cold pack pears for 10 minutes. Let set 5 minutes, then take out of water.

Syrup for Canning Fruit

Take a 1-gallon pitcher. Fill it ½ full of white sugar. Then fill pitcher with hot tap water. Stir until dissolved. Add more water if needed to fill pitcher. If you want it sweeter, adjust to your taste.

Pineapples to Can

Cut up pineapples (I prefer Dole) in tidbit size. You can do it by hand or use a pineapple slicer, then cut to tidbit size. Put pineapples in a bowl, add some sugar. Stir to dissolve sugar, it will make its own syrup. May need to add more sugar. Syrup should cover pineapples. Let stand 20–30 minutes. Put in jars and add the juice. If not enough to cover the pineapples, make some syrup (½ sugar, ½ water). Make sure syrup covers pineapples or they will turn brown. Cold pack 10 minutes. Take a spoon and scrape pineapple rinds. This gives you crushed pineapples to can or use it to make pie filling.

When cold packing:

Let all your jars set in the hot water for another 10 minutes before taking them out. Less messy jars, and juices will not come out from under your lids. Does a better sealing job.

Sweet Pickles (old-time favorite)

Soak 1 gallon sliced pickles in salt water (1 cup salt and enough cold water to cover). For 7 days: Drain off salt water and cover with boiling water. Next day, drain off water and cover again with fresh boiling water to which you add 1 tablespoon alum. Next day, drain and cover with fresh boiling water. Next day, drain again. Take 8 cups vinegar, 6 cups sugar, 2 tablespoons pickling spice; bring to a boil. Stir until sugar is dissolved. Pour over pickles. Next 4 days: drain off syrup, add 1 cup sugar each day. Reheat and pour over pickles. On day 4: Pack in jars; add syrup and cold pack.

My version: Put sliced pickles in a pot with a lid. Stir them every day, so there's no chance of mold forming on top. If it does, take a spoon and scoop it off.

You don't have to can these pickles. They keep indefinitely. Make sure syrup covers the pickles. Use the apple cider vinegar, if to tangy add some water and a little extra sugar. Put in glass or plastic gallon jars, push under your fruit cellar shelf, where it's dark and cool. They keep until next years pickling time. Take out only what you eat at one sitting. Use juice to make pickled eggs.

Sweet Dill

Spices:

½ tsp. dill weed

¼ tsp. alum

¼ tsp. turmeric

Syrup for 3 quart:

3 c. sugar

3 c. water

1 c. vinegar

1 Tbsp. salt

Put spices in a quart jar. Fill jar with sliced pickles, along with a few slices of onion. Bring the syrup to a boil and pour in pickle-filled jars. Cold pack, just until water starts to boil. Turn off heat, but do not remove lid. Let set until water is cold. Delicious!

Cinnamon Pickles

2 gal. lg. pickles—seeded, peeled and cut in bite-size pieces

Soak pickles in 8½ quart water and 2 cups lime for 24 hours. Drain and wash. Soak in cold water for 3 hours. Place in a kettle and simmer for 2 hours in the following solution: 1 cup vinegar, 1 small bottle red food coloring, 1 tablespoon alum and enough water to cover. When done, drain off the liquid. Meanwhile make a syrup of:

3 c. vinegar

6 cinnamon sticks

10 c. sugar

3 c. water

1 Tbsp. salt

10 oz. Brach's cinnamon candy discs

Crush discs—they will melt faster. Bring all syrup ingredients to a boil. Pour over pickles. Let set overnight and drain. Reheat this syrup every 24 hours for 3 days. On the 4th day, heat and can. I like to take smaller pickles, peel them and slice a little thicker than for sweet pickles instead of cutting into bite-size pieces. This recipe was created to use up the leftover, overgrown pickles.

Crispy Pickles

1 gal. sliced pickles

2 c. water

2 c. vinegar

4 c. sugar

Spices:

1 Tbsp. dill weed

1 Tbsp. celery seed

1 Tbsp. allspice

1 Tbsp. cinnamon

1 tsp. cloves

Put all the spices in a bag. Make a spice bag with a coffee filter, or a piece of muslin or organdy. Make sure your material is clean. Wash in clear water. No soap or fabric softener. To can pickles: add ½ cup salt to pickles and cover with water. Let set 3–5 days then drain. Add 1 tablespoon alum, cover with water, boil 10 minutes, drain again. Make syrup with the water, vinegar and sugar. Put the spice bag in it. Add the pickles and boil 10 minutes. Then put in jars and cold pack 10 minutes.

Freezer Pickles

14 c. shredded or sliced pickles

2 green peppers, sliced

2 lb. onions, sliced

1 c. chopped celery

½ c. salt

3 c. sugar

2 c. vinegar

Mix all together. Let set overnight. Put in containers and freeze.

Corn Sauce

8 c. fresh corn (12 ears)

6 c. shredded cabbage

6 stalks celery, chopped

2 c. chopped green peppers

2 c. chopped red peppers

1 lb. carrots, sliced

Cook corn as you would for corn on the cob. Cool in cold water. Cut off the kernels. Cook the rest of the vegetables until tender. Drain off the water. Put all in a stockpot. Add vinegar and sugar syrup. Cook a few minutes. You can keep in the refrigerator a day or two, and check the taste. By then the syrup should be soaked in. You can add more sugar and vinegar to your taste. Reheat and put in jars, cold pack 20 minutes. Serve with a meal.

Tomato Cocktail

8 qt. tomato juice

8 stalks celery

1 bunch parsley

2 c. chopped onions

2 c. chopped peppers

1 c. sugar

Cook until vegetables are tender; put in jars and cold pack 20 minutes. I like to put the vegetables through a fine, hand-cranked grinder. I use tomato cocktail in every recipe that asks for tomato juice. It has a more satisfying taste. Give it a try.

Green Tomato Relish

1 peck green tomatoes

1 (5 lb.) head cabbage

8 onions

½ c. salt

3 red peppers

3 green peppers

6 stalks celery

½ oz. turmeric

½ oz. celery seed

1 oz. mustard seed

3 lb. sugar

3 pt. vinegar

Chop or grind first 3 ingredients, add salt and let set 4–5 hours. Squeeze out all the juice (discard). Chop or grind peppers and celery. Heat vinegar and sugar until melted. Add all ingredients and cook together 15 minutes. Put in jars and cold pack 15 minutes. Very good on roasted hot dogs. Why green tomatoes? Try it, you just might like it. Created to use up the last veggies in your fall garden.

Tomato Relish

(Fox hunter's delight) When Grandpa joined his buddies for a night of fox chasing. Sitting by the fire, way past midnight, enjoying a roasted hot dog with their favorite relish.

1 peck tomatoes (I prefer Roma)

2½ c. sugar

½ tsp. ketchup spice or to suit your taste

¼ c. mustard

¼ c. vinegar

1½ tsp. salt

¼ c. chopped onions

¼ c. chopped red peppers

¼ c. chopped green peppers

¼ c. chopped sweet pickles

Combine sugar, spice, mustard, vinegar and salt. Cook together until slightly thickened, stirring frequently. Meanwhile chop onions, peppers and pickles. Peel tomatoes and remove some of the seeds, chop tomatoes. When first mixture is cooked (about 10 minutes) add all the rest of the ingredients except pickles. Cook until slightly thickened. Remove from heat, cool slightly, add pickles. Cold pack 20 minutes.

Tomato Ketchup

1 peck tomatoes (8 qt. juice)

3 lg. onions

1 pt. vinegar

4 c. sugar

3 Tbsp. salt

½ oz. ketchup spice

Cook tomatoes and onions until soft, then put through sieve. Drain in jelly bag and throw away juice. Bring pulp to a boil, add the rest of ingredients. Cook 10 minutes and seal in ½ pint jars.

My version: Drain tomato juice 12 hours. Blend onions, use juice and all. I use 1½ cup blended onions, 3 tablespoons ketchup spice, same amount sugar, vinegar and salt as in the recipe above. Add ½ package Mrs. Wages ketchup mix. Cook 10 minutes or until desired thickness. Put in ½ pint jars and cold pack 10 minutes. Let set another 15 minutes.

Salsa

4 qt. chopped tomatoes (Roma work best)

2 green peppers

3 c. chopped onions

3 hot peppers

6 banana peppers

a handful of fresh parsley

2 Tbsp. sugar

3 Tbsp. salt

1 Tbsp. ReaLemon

1 tsp. minced garlic or garlic powder

Chop all vegetables with Kitchen Plus 2000 Salsa Master, or cut tomatoes by hand. I don't peel. Put first 6 ingredients in Stanley roaster and add the rest of ingredients. Cook for 1 hour. If too thin, thicken with Perma Flo mixed with water. Add enough until desired thickness. Spoon in jars and seal. Yield: 17 - ½ pint jars. If I don't have banana peppers, I use all hot peppers. I add ⅓ cup brown sugar, 2 tablespoons taco seasoning.

Add ½ teaspoon salt and ½ teaspoon ReaLemon juice to each pint when canning vegetables. When I do this, I have no problem with jars becoming unsealed and spoiled.

230

Dressing to Freeze

52 c. bread cubes (4 loaves homemade bread)

2 c. chicken broth

3 Tbsp. chicken base

2 Tbsp. salt

1 Tbsp. pepper

6 c. diced carrots

4 c. chopped celery

2 c. chopped onions

4 c. cubed chicken, cooked

4 c. diced potatoes

5 qt. milk

12 eggs, beaten

fresh parsley, chopped; or dry parsley flakes, optional

Mix all together in a 13 quart mixing bowl, adding toasted bread cubes last. Mix in the early morning, then let set until in the afternoon or overnight, if you have room in the refrigerator. Stir occasionally. Put 3 tablespoons butter in your skillet and melt before adding the dressing to fry. Fill the skillet, but not overflowing. Stir and flip dressing and fry to desired doneness. The old iron skillet still works best for me. When done put on cookie sheets to cool. When cold put in freezer boxes and freeze. To serve: Put frozen dressing in a casserole or pan, put in the oven on low heat until partly thawed. Take a fork and break apart. Turn oven to 350° and bake until heated thoroughly. Serve with your meal. Recipe for the toasted bread cubes in Breads and Rolls section.

Hamburger Crumbles to Can

Put hamburger in a skillet (no butter), add chopped onions or onion salt and other seasonings to your taste. Fry till nice and brown. Put in a colander to drain grease.

Or, you can bake the hamburger instead: Put hamburger on a cookie sheet, add your seasonings and bake at 350°, turning occasionally. Bake to desired doneness. Drain grease.

Chop until no big chunks remain. Pack into pint jars. Cold pack 2 hours. Pack into jars real tight or jars will float in your canner. This hamburger can be used in any dish you prepare. It is very handy.

Meatballs to Can or Freeze

3 lb. hamburger

2 c. oatmeal

2 eggs

½ c. milk

5 oz. evaporated milk

2 Tbsp. chopped onions or ½ tsp. onion salt

2 tsp. salt

½ tsp. garlic salt

½ tsp. pepper

Sauce:

2 c. ketchup

1 c. brown sugar

½ tsp. garlic salt

⅓ tsp. liquid hickory smoke

2 Tbsp. Worcestershire sauce

1 Tbsp. ReaLemon

1 c. barbecue sauce

Form meatballs using #40 cookie or ice cream scoop. Place one layer of meatballs on a cookie sheet and bake at 325° for 1 hour, turning the meatballs at ½ hour. Put meatballs in quart jars or freezer containers. Add 1 cup sauce. If you have extra sauce, divide among jars. Cold pack 3 hours. Yield: 8 quart.

Beef Bologna

(old-time favorite)

100 lb. meat cuttings for hamburger

4 lb. Tender Quick

1 lb. brown sugar

½ lb. salt

3 oz. black pepper

1 oz. salt petre

20 lb. water

Mix dry ingredients with meat. Let set overnight and grind. Then mix in water. (Let set for 3 days in a cold place.) Stuff in wide-mouth jars. Cold pack 3 hours. We like to start out with hamburger since we don't have a meat grinder, and it is less hassle. Slice about ½" thick in your jar, take pieces out one by one. Roll in flour, then fry in butter. Serve with mashed potatoes and a vegetable. Or, use to make sandwiches. If you use 1½ pint wide-mouth jars, you should be able to slide meat out of jar before you slice. It's easier than the quart jars.

Canning Chicken

Use boneless, skinless chicken breasts, chicken tenders, or boneless leg quarters. Dust in Runion breading mix, fry in butter, season with Lawry's until golden brown. Put in wide-mouth jars. Fill with water. Cold pack 2½ hours. When you want to serve it: heat chicken along with the juice in the jar. Once it is hot you have chicken and gravy to serve with your potatoes.

Pizza Sauce

7 qt. tomato juice
4 c. chopped onions
½ c. butter
1 c. sugar
1 c. brown sugar
½ c. Perma Flo
3 (12 oz.) cans tomato paste
3 (6.5 oz.) cans mushrooms, chopped
4 tsp. salt
1 tsp. pepper
2 Tbsp. pizza spice
1 tsp. oregano
1 tsp. chili powder
2 tsp. Creole seasoning
2 tsp. Chipotle Tabasco sauce
1 Tbsp. garlic salt
½ pkg. Mrs. Wages pizza sauce mix, optional

Fry chopped onions in butter in large stainless steel canner or stock pot. Add all of the other ingredients and simmer 1 hour. Put in jars. Cold pack 15 minutes.

When making chili soup, sloppy joe, pizza sauce, etc., you have added all the ingredients but something doesn't taste right . . . add some brown sugar. That usually adds the finished taste.

Pizza Sauce

8 qt. tomato juice
3 onions, chopped
1½–2 c. sugar
2 Tbsp. salt
6 Tbsp. flour
1 Tbsp. oregano
2 tsp. garlic powder
2 tsp. pepper
1 c. Wesson oil

Cook together for 20 minutes. Put in jars and cold pack 15 minutes.

Spaghetti Sauce

6 lb. hamburger
12 qt. tomato juice
3 c. chopped onions
5 Tbsp. chili powder
2 Tbsp. mustard
black pepper, salt and sugar to taste

Fry hamburger and onions until brown. Add tomato juice and seasonings. Cold pack 45 minutes.

My version of seasoning added:
1 Tbsp. black pepper
¼ c. salt
3 c. brown sugar
¼ c. Lawry's
5 Tbsp. Southwest Chipotle seasoning

Chili Soup

10 lb. hamburger
4 c. chopped onions
3 c. flour
6 qt. tomato juice, divided
3 c. brown sugar
2 c. homemade ketchup, optional
2 envelopes McCormick Chili seasoning
1½ gal. kidney beans

In a 20 qt. stock pot, fry hamburger and onions until hamburger is no longer red. Do not drain. Add 2 quart tomato juice and flour; mix well. Add the rest of ingredients. Leave beans until last. I like to add some chili beans and some Southwest Chipotle seasoning. Add enough water to make 5 gallons soup. I use all tomato juice (10 quart) in addition to the first 6 quart. Heat thoroughly, and put in jars. Cold pack 2 hours.

Vegetable Soup

5 lb. frozen vegetables
5 lb. hamburger, fried
½ c. sugar
8 c. diced celery
8 c. chopped onions
10 c. cubed potatoes
3 (46 oz.) cans beef broth
2 (46 oz.) cans tomato juice
8 tsp. beef bouillon
salt, pepper and seasoned salt to taste

Heat everything together in a large canner. Add water if desired. By heating, it brings out the flavor. Add more spices if needed. Cold pack 2½ hours. Yield: 18–20 quart.

Vegetable Soup

Put 5 lb. chunk meat in a pot, cover with water. Cook over medium heat until meat is tender. Drain off broth and save, add enough water to make 6 qt. If you have more than 6 qt. before adding water—good—use it all.

Add:

7½ lb. frozen mixed vegetables

6 qt. tomato cocktail

16 oz. beef base dissolved in 1 qt. hot water

Add meat back into mixture. No other seasonings needed.

Bean with Bacon Soup

3 lb. bacon

4 c. chopped onions

6 qt. tomato juice

1½ c. brown sugar

2 tsp. pepper

3 bay leaves

seasonings to taste

16 oz. canned navy beans or pork and beans

6 c. chopped celery

8 c. cubed potatoes

4 c. chopped carrots

Fry bacon, remove bacon and crumble. Fry onions in bacon grease. Pour into a 20 quart stock pot. Add tomato juice, sugar and seasonings; bring to a boil. Add vegetables, bring to a boil. Simmer 10 minutes. Remove bag leaves. Put in jars and cold pack 2½ hours. I like to fry bacon and the onions in iron skillet.

Beans for Soup

Soak navy beans in cold water overnight. Drain. Fill your jars ¾ full with beans and fill jar with hot water. Cold pack for 3 hours.

Sauerkraut to Can

Shred cabbage as you do for slaw. Press tightly in pint jars. Punch a hole in the middle with handle of a wooden spoon. Put 1 teaspoon vinegar, ½ teaspoon salt and ½ teaspoon sugar in the hole. Fill jar with boiling water. Screw lid on lightly and let set 6 weeks to ferment. Ready to use, or cold pack for 30 minutes.

Stew in the Kettle

½ c. butter

2 qt. beef chunks or hamburger

1 sm. onion, chopped

6 c. water

salt and pepper to taste

Lawry's seasoned salt

16 c. mixed vegetables

Start your fire under the tripod, hang on your iron kettle (2–3 gal. kettle). Melt butter, add meat and onion. Fry until meat is browned and tender. Add water and some seasonings. Bring to a boil, add vegetables, cook until tender. Serve right out of the kettle. Cool leftovers completely. Freeze in serving-size containers. An easy and quick meal for 2 or for unexpected company. Serve with a salad. Fresh vegetables can be used instead, but longer cooking is required.

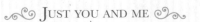

Barbecued Peppers and Onions

1 qt. pizza sauce (homemade)

1 Tbsp. salt

6 oz. ketchup

1 c. vinegar

2 c. sugar

1½ c. vegetable oil

2 qt. cut-up onions

2 qt. red and green peppers

Bring first 6 ingredients to a boil for 10 minutes. Add onions and peppers. Cook 1–3 minutes. Pour into jars while hot. Cold pack just to the boiling point. Turn heat off and let set until cold. Serve on scrambled eggs, roasted hot dogs, hamburger sandwiches, pizza, etc.

Hot Pepper Butter

36 hot peppers (6 cups ground)

4 c. mustard

4 c. vinegar

1 Tbsp. salt

3 c. sugar

1½ c. flour

2 c. water

Mix flour and water. Add to the rest of ingredients and cook until thick. Cold pack 15 minutes. I take about ½ of the pepper seeds out. If you like it hotter, leave the seeds in. Use on barbecued burgers.

Hot Pepper Jelly

2 green peppers
3 red peppers
10 hot peppers
1 box Sure-Jell
1 c. vinegar
5 c. sugar
1 Tbsp. butter

Grind or blend the peppers. Put in a saucepan and add Sure-Jell and vinegar, bring to a boil. Add sugar, boil 1 minute. Take off heat, add butter. Stir until dissolved. Spoon in ½ pint jars. Cold pack 10 minutes. Mix 1 jar with an 8 ounce bar cream cheese and serve with crackers. Or put cream cheese on a plate and pour jelly over cream cheese. Can be used as an appetizer.

Zucchini Relish

5 c. chopped zucchini
2 c. chopped onions
2½ Tbsp. salt
1 sweet red pepper, chopped
1½ c. sugar
1 Tbsp. clear jel
1½ tsp. turmeric
1 tsp. dry mustard
¼ tsp. pepper
1 c. cider vinegar
1 tsp. celery seed

Combine zucchini, onions and salt. Let set overnight. Rinse and drain well. Combine all ingredients in a large kettle and cook until mixture thickens. Stir constantly. Put in jars. Cold pack 10 minutes.

Homemade Cheese Whiz

3 lb. Velveeta cheese

¾ c. evaporated milk or cream

2 c. milk

½ c. margarine (Blue Bonnet)

Melt together over low heat. Put in ½ pint jars and cold pack 20 minutes. Serve with crackers.

Strawberry Jam

5 c. mashed strawberries

7 c. sugar

⅓ c. Sure-Jell (bulk) or 1 box Sure-Jell

½ tsp. butter

Take 2 quart fresh strawberries, remove stems, wash and drain. Mash strawberries, and measure into 6 quart saucepan. Measure sugar into a mixing bowl. Set aside. Add Sure-Jell to strawberries and bring to a rolling boil. Add butter to prevent foaming during cooking. Stir constantly. Add sugar quickly. Bring to a rolling boil and boil exactly 1 minute, stirring constantly. Remove from heat. Skim off foam. Fill jars immediately. Screw on lids tightly. Invert jars 5 minutes, then turn upright. Yield: 9 - ½ pint jars. Any jars not sealed can be stored in refrigerator until ready to use.

Quince Honey

1 c. chopped quince

1 c. chopped apples

1 c. water

4 c. sugar

Wash and core quince and apples. Grate or grind both fruits and mix together. Add water to fruit and bring to a boil. Gradually add sugar, stir until all sugar has dissolved. Cook slowly until fruit is clear and mixture is thick (about 15 minutes). Pour in jars and seal.

Raspberry Jelly

5 c. tomato juice

4 c. sugar

1 box Sure-Jell

1 (6 oz.) box red raspberry Jell-O

Bring first 3 ingredients to a hard boil; boil 15 minutes. Add red raspberry Jell-O, stir until fully dissolved. Cool. Refrigerate or put in small jars. Yes, this recipe is correct. Tomato juice is the correct ingredient.

Pear Butter

4 c. mashed pears

8 c. sugar

2 c. crushed pineapple

 Or:

4 c. mashed pears

2 c. sugar

2 c. Karo

Combine all ingredients in a saucepan. Bring to a rolling boil and boil about 15 minutes, until it reads 220° on the thermometer. Stir constantly so it will not scorch. Put jars and lids in hot water until ready to fill. When filled and lid is on, turn upside down until cold. No need to cold pack.

When making jams and jellies, always have your jars and lids in hot water, until you are ready to fill and seal your jars.

Grape Butter

5 c. grapes

5 c. sugar

2 Tbsp. water

½ c. Karo

Boil 20 minutes, then put through food mill to remove seeds. Bring to a boil again. Put in jars and seal. Serve with homemade bread.

Rhubarb Juice

2 qt. rhubarb, cut up

2¼ c. sugar

1 pkg. strawberry or strawberry kiwi Kool-Aid

2 c. pineapple juice

½ c. ReaLemon

Cover rhubarb with water and boil 10 minutes. Put through colander, let drip at least 1 hour. Take 2 quart juice (if not enough, add water), melt sugar in 2 cups water. Add Kool-Aid, pineapple juice and ReaLemon. Put in pint jars and cold pack 10 minutes. Yield: 2 gallons. When ready to serve, add 1 can Sprite or 7-Up to a pint of rhubarb juice.

Frozen Lemonade

1 (12 qt.) Country Time lemonade mix
1 pkg. lemon Kool-Aid
1 c. sugar
8 qt. cold water
4 lemon halves, squeezed
7-Up or Sprite
lemon and lime slices

Mix first 5 ingredients, stir until sugar is dissolved. Put in pint or quart containers and freeze. To serve, thaw slightly, add I can 7-Up per pint of lemonade. Take two thin slices lemon and lime and cut into 4–6 pieces. Add to lemonade, serve while slushy. For a larger group: freeze in 4 quart ice cream pail. Add 2-liter of 7-Up, garnish with lemons and limes to your desire. Very refreshing. Don't worry about leftovers. There are usually none.

Buy 4 oz. spice bowls with lids at the bulk food store. Put shredded cheese and sloppy joe in bowls and freeze. Ideal for lunch box salad. Or, if you want a quick salad when you're home by yourself.

Tea Concentrate

(tea party time)

2 c. sugar

2 c. tea leaves (packed)

4 c. boiling water

Pour boiling water over tea leaves and sugar in a stainless steel mixing bowl (not plastic). Let set 6–7 hours. Squeeze all juice out of leaves. Strain tea. Use 1 cup frozen concentrate to 2 quart cold water. Enjoy a glass of iced tea.

Frozen Fruit Slush

3 c. water

2 c. sugar

1 qt. chopped, fresh peaches

20 oz. crushed pineapple

6 oz. orange juice concentrate

6 lg. bananas, sliced

Bring water and sugar to a boil. Set aside to cool. Mix the rest of ingredients together in a large mixing bowl. Add cooled sugar water. Yield: 28 - ½ cup servings. Foam cups with lids may be purchased at your local bulk food store or use freezer boxes.

Frozen Strawberries, (tasting fresh)

Wash, hull and drain strawberries. Put in single layers on paper towels until dry. Put whole strawberries in containers and freeze. When ready to use, chop strawberries and add desired amount of sugar. Have fresh-tasting strawberries all winter long.

5 Alive Peaches

(to can or freeze)
6 qt. sliced peaches
2 c. sugar
⅓ c. Tang
½ c. 5 Alive concentrate
2 Tbsp. fruit fresh or 1 Tbsp. Vitamin C powder

Sprinkle all dry ingredients over peach slices. Mix well, when dissolved add 5 Alive. Let set at least 15 minutes before you put in freezer boxes. Makes its own juice. When canning the peaches you may need to add a little extra syrup so all peaches are covered. Make syrup with equal amounts of sugar and water and divide among your jars. Cold pack: when it comes to a rolling boil, time for 7 minutes. Turn off heat and let set 10 minutes, remove from the hot water. But are best when frozen.

Freeze leftover fruit juice. When you have
enough, thaw, cook and slightly thicken
with clear jel. Add different fresh fruits. A
refreshing dessert.

JUST YOU AND ME

Backyard Gatherings

Morning Tea Party

10:00 AM

Invited 10–12 friends

Everyone bring their own cup and saucer.

If you're outside, have a pot of hot water hanging over the open fire.

Have an assortment of tea bags and/or have your kitchen shears ready.

Have them clip their own tea from your garden. Have each tea patch labeled.

Have each person bring a finger food beginning with the first letter of their name.

Serve your guests—using different plates or napkins for everybody.

Things to do:

Sit around the open fire, enjoy your food and friendship.

Give a prize for the first or last person that arrived.

Have your guests vote on the prettiest cup and saucer.

Play guessing games: fill a small peanut butter jar with macaroni, marshmallows, chocolate chips, etc. For the prize: a dozen cookies or a box of tea bags.

Give them a pen and paper, answer the questions yourself as you read them to your guests. Have them answer questions about yourself:

Examples:

1. What is my favorite color?

2. What time did I get up?

3. Favorite flower?

4. How many children do I have?

5. Favorite time of year?

See who has the most answers like yourself.

Morning or Afternoon Tea Party

Invite friends

Greet them with a pitcher of orange juice, iced tea, or a pot of hot tea.

Use all different glasses and tea cups.

Have your guests sit around the table, each setting may be different, or serve buffet style.

Take an old vase or pitcher and fix a bouquet of cut flowers from your garden for a centerpiece.

Put a sticker on the bottom of one glass. After your guests are done eating, whoever has the sticker gets to take home the centerpiece.

If your food isn't quite ready when they arrive, have them fill their glass or cup and take a stroll through the yard and garden until you're ready.

After your guests have been seated, ask God's grace with a bow of silence. Pick up the plates and fix up with your prepared food. Serve your guests.

Be creative, use your imagination. Any way is right!

Garden Tea Party

1. How many words can you make with these letters only (Garden Tea party). Give them 5 minutes. Example: den, neat, yard, near, part, dear, ten, garter.

2. Bring your oldest broom. Have your guests vote for the ugliest broom, and give a new soft-sweep broom.

3. Scramble names of flowers or vegetables. Example: ppypo = poppy; sreso = roses; ynspa = pansy; ncro = corn; naesb = beans; ttaoom = tomato

Grandpa always said: Winter will not set in until the ponds are full and the ditches are cleaned out. Still holds true today.

JUST YOU AND ME

Evening Party - Tea or Coffee

Have an outdoor fire with a pot of hot water for tea or a pot of coffee (or both). This does not have to be ladies only. Let them bring their better halves too.

Have kerosene lanterns hanging and lit throughout the yard, especially around the tables where you will be serving your guests.

Have finger foods and snacks to pass around while sitting around the open fire.

You can have a question and answer game about yourself and husband or simply enjoy your friendship around the open fire.

Roast hot dogs, have all sorts of toppings for your hot dogs—sloppy joe, chopped onions, chopped tomatoes, chopped lettuce, etc. Serve with fresh fruit and assorted dips, or frozen fruits mixed with blueberries and a sprig of mint tea from your garden. Also potato chips, an assortment of cookies, and have each lady bring 1 dozen of her favorite cookies. Be sure to serve s'mores (roasted marshmallows between 2 fudge stripe cookies).

Plant a Cheerful Garden

First plant 5 rows of peas:

piety, prudence, prayer, praise, purity

Next plant 5 rows of squash:

squash gossip, squash idleness, squash pride, squash unkindness, squash self-indulgence

Then plant 5 rows of lettuce:

let-us-be-humble, let-us-be-faithful, let-us-be-unselfish, let-us-be-loving, let-us-be-sanctified

And to make all things count for something good and worthwhile, no garden is complete without turnips:

turn-up-for-church-services

turn-up-to-go-the-second-mile

turn-up-with-a-cheerful-smile

turn-up-with-a-willing-mind

Ideas

I like to buy old and odd pieces of glassware at flea markets or garage sales. You do not have to spend a lot of money. Keep it simple.

You want to eat outside. Set up a small table with 2-4 chairs at different places on the porch or flower garden, or put everyone at the picnic table.

Take old quart jars, put 1–2" sand or small gravel in the bottom. Put a tea light or a votive cup with a candle in the jar. Set around and light the candles when almost dark. Surprising how much light you will have.

Solar lights scattered throughout the yard and garden or citronella torches or candles, etc., will light your paths after dark.

Hang an old chandelier from a tree or under the awning, glue ½ pint jars to the candle sockets, put a votive or tea light in each jar.

You can find recipes throughout the cookbook that will work for your outdoor gatherings.

Buy baskets at garage sales or Goodwill. They may be painted with spray paint. Line with a plastic grocery bag. Plant flowers in them to decorate for your backyard gatherings. Also nice to give as gifts.

Stick small solar lights in flower pots on patio.

Index

Finale

May a blessing be upon the cook
Who sees and buys this little book.
And buying, tries and tests its wares;
While testing throws away her cares;
And carefree, tells her neighbor cook
To get another such a book.

JUST YOU AND ME

Desserts

Cakes, Cookies, Bars & Frostings

Pies

Just you and me

Index